OCCASIONAL PAPERS SERIES 1

MAQĀṢID AL-SHARĪʿAH
A BEGINNER'S GUIDE

JASSER AUDA

THE INTERNATIONAL INSTITUTE OF ISLAMIC THOUGHT
LONDON · WASHINGTON

THE INTERNATIONAL INSTITUTE OF ISLAMIC THOUGHT
LONDON OFFICE
P.O. BOX 126, RICHMOND, SURREY TW9 2UD, UK
WWW.IIITUK.COM

USA OFFICE
P.O. BOX 669, HERNDON, VA 20172, USA
WWW.IIIT.ORG

ISBN 978-1-56564-440-3

Typesetting by Shiraz Khan
Diagrams by Sideek Ali
Printed in the United Kingdom by Cromwell Press

SERIES EDITORS
DR. ANAS S. AL SHAIKH-ALI
SHIRAZ KHAN

CONTENTS

FOREWORD

The International Institute of Islamic Thought (IIIT) has great pleasure in presenting this guide introducing the subject of *Maqāṣid al-Sharīʿah*, the higher objectives and intents of Islamic Law. The author, Dr. Jasser Auda, is a well-known multi-disciplinary scholar, who has developed a specialization in this field.

Since few works in the English language have been available on the subject of *Maqāṣid al-Sharīʿah,* the IIIT decided to fill the vaccum by initiating the translation and publication of a series of books on *al-Maqāṣid* to introduce this important and difficult area of thought to English readers. These include to date, *Ibn Ashur Treatise on Maqāṣid al-Shariʿah*, *Imam al-Shāṭibī's Theory of the Higher Objectives and Intents of Islamic Law* by Ahmad al-Raysuni, *Towards Realization of the Higher Intents of Islamic Law: Maqāṣid al-Shariʿah a Functional Approach* by Gamal Eldin Attia, and *Maqasid al-Shariʿah as Philosophy of Islamic Law: A Systems Approach* by Jasser Auda.

As the topic is complex and intellectually challenging, with most books appearing on the subject written mainly for specialists, scholars and intellectuals alone, the IIIT London Office is also producing other simple introductory guides to the subject as part of its Occasional Papers series with a view to providing easy accessible material for the general reader. These include *Maqāṣid al-Sharīʿah Made Simple* by Muhammad Hashim Kamali, and *The Islamic Vision of Development in the Light of Maqāṣid al-Sharīʿah* by Muhammad Umer Chapra.

ANAS S. AL SHAIKH-ALI
Academic Advisor, IIIT London Office

(1)
WHAT IS *MAQĀṢID*?

Levels of Why

Children often come up with deep philosophical questions, and one cannot tell whether they mean these questions or not! However, the beauty of a child's question is that it is often not bound by pre-set 'facts' or 'this is the way things are' logic. I often start courses on *Maqāṣid al-Sharīʿah* with the story of a little girl who asked her father: 'Dad, why do you stop the car at the traffic light?' Her father replied, with an educative tone: 'Because the light is red, and red means stop.' The girl asked: 'But why?' The Dad replied also with a tone of education: 'So the policeman does not give us a ticket.' The girl went on: 'But why would the policeman give us a ticket?' The Dad answered: 'Well. Because crossing a red light is dangerous.' The girl continued: 'Why?' Now the Dad thought of saying: 'This is the way things are,' but then decided to be a bit philosophical with his little beloved daughter. Thus, he answered: 'Because we cannot hurt people. Would you like to be hurt yourself?' The girl said: 'No!' The dad said: 'And people also do not want to be hurt. The Prophet (peace be upon him) said: "Love for people what you love for yourself."' But instead of stopping there, the girl asked: 'Why do you love for people what you love for yourself?' After a bit of thinking, the father said: 'Because all people are equal, and if you would like to ask why, I would say that God is The Just, and out of His Justice, He made us all equal, with equal rights, and that is the way He made the world!'

The question of 'why' is equivalent to the question of 'what is the *maqāṣid*?' And the 'levels of why,' as philosophers have put it, are the 'levels of *maqāṣid*,' as Islamic jurists have put it. These levels of why and the exploration of *maqāṣid* will take us from the details of simple actions, and clear 'signs', such as stopping at a red traffic light, from the level of actions and signs to the level of laws and regulations, such as traffic laws, from the level of laws and regulations to the level of mutual benefits and 'utility', such as people's consideration of others' safety in exchange of their own safety, and finally, from the level of benefits and utility to the level of the overall principles and basic beliefs, such as justice, compassion, and the attributes of God.

Therefore, *maqāṣid al-sharīʿah* is the branch of Islamic knowledge that answers all the challenging questions of 'why' on various levels, such as the following questions:

- *Why is giving charity (zakah) one of Islam's principle 'pillars'?*
- *Why is it an Islamic obligation to be good to your neighbors?*
- *Why do Muslims greet people with salam (peace)?*
- *Why do Muslims have to pray several times every day?*
- *Why is fasting during the month of Ramadan one of Islam's principle 'pillars'?*
- *Why do Muslims mention the name of God all the time?*
- *Why is drinking any amount of alcohol a major sin in Islam?*
- *Why is smoking weed, for example, as prohibited as drinking alcohol in Islam?*
- *Why is the death penalty a (maximum) punishment in the Islamic law for rape or genocide?*

Maqāṣid al-sharīʿah explain the 'wisdoms behind rulings,' such as 'enhancing social cohesion,' which is one of the wisdoms behind charity, being good to one's neighbors, and greeting people with peace.

Wisdoms behind rulings also include 'developing consciousness of God,' which is one of the rationales behind regular prayers, fasting, and supplications.

Maqāṣid are also good ends that the laws aim to achieve by blocking, or opening, certain means. Thus, the *maqāṣid* of 'preserving the minds and souls of people' explain the total and strict Islamic ban on alcohol and intoxicants, and the *maqāṣid* of 'protecting people's property and honor' explain the Qur'an's mentioning of a 'death penalty' as a (possible) punishment for rape or genocide (interpretations of verses 2:178 and 5:33, according to a number of schools of Islamic law).

Maqāṣid are also the group of divine intents and moral concepts upon which the Islamic law is based, such as justice, human dignity, free will, magnanimity, chastity, facilitation, and social cooperation. Thus, they represent the link between the Islamic law and today's notions of human rights, development, and civility, and could answer some other type of questions, such as:

- *What is the best methodology for re-reading and re-interpreting the Islamic scripture in light of today's realities?*
- *What is the Islamic concept of 'freedom' and 'justice'?*
- *What is the link between today's notions of human rights and Islamic law?*
- *How can Islamic law contribute to 'development,' morality, and 'civility'?*

Let us, next, study the terminology and theory of *maqāṣid* more formally.

'Maqāṣid' and 'Maṣāliḥ'

The term '*maqṣid*' (plural: *maqāṣid*) refers to a purpose, objective, principle, intent, goal, end,[1] telos (Greek), finalité (French), or Zweck (German).[2] *Maqāṣid* of the Islamic law are the objectives/purposes/intents/ends/principles behind the Islamic rulings.[3] For a number of Islamic legal theorists, it is an alternative expression to 'people's interests' (*maṣāliḥ*). For example, ʿAbd al-Malik al-Juwaynī (d. 478 AH/1185 CE), one of the earliest contributors to *al-maqāṣid* theory as we know it today (as will be explained shortly) used *al-maqāṣid* and public interests (*al-maṣāliḥ al-ʿāmmah*) interchangeably.[4] Abū Ḥāmid al-Ghazālī (d. 505 AH/1111 CE) elaborated on a classification of *maqāṣid*, which he placed entirely under what he called 'unrestricted interests' (*al-maṣāliḥ al-mursalah*).[5] Fakhr al-Dīn al-Rāzī (d. 606 AH/1209 CE) and al-Āmidī (d. 631 AH/1234 CE) followed al-Ghazālī in his terminology.[6] Najm al-Dīn al-Ṭūfī (d.716 AH/1316 CE), defined *maṣlaḥah* as, 'what fulfills the purpose of the Legislator.'[7] Al-Qarāfī (d. 1285 AH/1868 CE) linked *maṣlaḥah* and *maqāṣid* by a fundamental (*uṣūlī*) 'rule' that stated: 'A purpose (*maqṣid*) is not valid unless it leads to the fulfilment of some good (*maṣlaḥah*) or the avoidance of some mischief (*mafsadah*).'[8] Therefore, a *maqṣid*, purpose, objective, principle, intent, goal, end, or principle in the Islamic law is there for the 'interest of humanity.' This is the rational basis, if you wish, for the *maqāṣid* theory.

Dimensions of Maqāṣid

Purposes or *maqāṣid* of the Islamic law themselves are classified in various ways, according to a number of dimensions. The following are some of these dimensions:

1. Levels of necessity, which is the traditional classification.
2. Scope of the rulings aiming to achieve purposes.
3. Scope of people included in purposes.
4. Level of universality of the purposes.

Traditional classifications of *maqāṣid* divide them into three 'levels of necessity,' which are7 necessities (*ḍarūrāt*), needs (*ḥājiyāt*), and luxuries (*taḥsīniyyāt*). Necessities are further classified into what 'preserves one's faith, soul, wealth, mind, and offspring.'[9] Some jurists added 'the preservation of honor' to the above five widely popular necessities.[10] These necessities were considered essential matters for human life itself. Thus, human life is in jeopardy if the minds of people are in jeopardy. That is why Islam is strict about banning alcohol and intoxicants. Human life is also in jeopardy if no measures are taken to protect people's 'souls' by protecting their health and their environment. That is why the Prophet Muhammad (ṢAAS)*prohibited all shapes and forms of 'harm' to another human being, other animals, or even plants. Human life is also in danger

*(ṢAAS) – *Ṣallā Allāhu ʿalayhi wa sallam*. May the peace and blessings of God be upon him. Said whenever the name of Prophet Muhammad is mentioned.

when in the case of financial (i.e. economic) crisis. That is why Islam bans monopoly, usury, and all shapes and forms of corruption and fraud. The high status given to the preservation of 'offspring' here also explains the many Islamic rulings that regulate and promote an excellent education and kind care for children. Finally, the 'preservation of faith' is a necessity for human life, albeit in the afterlife sense! Islam looks at life as a journey, part of which is on this earth and the rest of it is indeed in the afterlife! There is also a general agreement that the preservation of these necessities is the 'objective behind any revealed law,'[11] not just the Islamic law.

Purposes at the level of needs are less essential for human life. Examples of this are marriage, trade, and means of transportation. Islam encourages and regulates these needs. However, the lack of any of these needs is not a matter of life and death, especially on an individual basis. Human life, as a whole, in not in danger if some individuals choose not to marry or travel. However, if the lack of any of these 'needs' becomes widespread, then they move from the level of needs to the level of necessities. The fundamental rule in the Islamic law states: 'A need that is widespread should be treated as a necessity.'

Purposes at the level of luxuries are 'beautifying purposes,' such as using perfume, stylish clothing, and beautiful homes. These are things that Islam encourages, and considers to be further signs and proofs for God's endless mercy and generosity with human beings, but also asserts how they should take a lower priority in one's life.

The levels in the hierarchy are overlapping and interrelated, so noticed Imam al-Shāṭibī (who will be introduced shortly). In addition, each level should serve the level(s) below.[12] For example, both marriage and trade (from the level of needs) serve, and are highly related with, the necessities of the preservation of offsprings and wealth. And so on. Therefore, the general lack of one item from a certain level moves it to the level above. For example, the decline of trade on a global level, i.e. during the time of global economic crises, moves 'trade' from a 'need' into a 'life necessity,' and so on. That is why some jurists preferred to perceive necessities in terms of 'overlapping circles,' rather than a strict hierarchy.[13] See following chart.

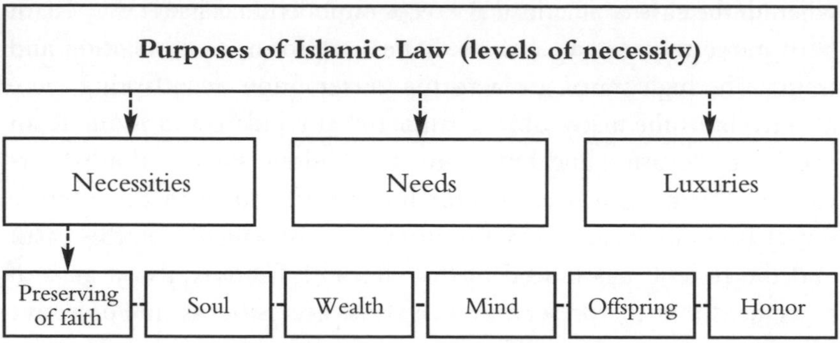

Hierarchy of the purposes of the Islamic law (dimension of levels of necessity)

I find the levels of necessity reminiscent of the twentieth century's Abraham Maslow's hierarchy of human (rather than 'divine') objectives or 'basic goals,' which he called, 'hierarchy of needs.'[14] Human needs, according to Maslow, range from basic physiological requirements and safety, to love and esteem, and, finally, 'self-actualisation.' In 1943, Maslow suggested five levels for these needs. Then, in 1970, he revised his ideas and suggested a seven level hierarchy.[15] The similarity between al-Shāṭibī's and Maslow's theory in terms of the levels of goals is interesting. Moreover, the second version of Maslow's theory reveals another interesting similarity with Islamic 'goal' theories, which is the capacity to evolve with time.

Islamic theories of goals (*maqāṣid*) evolved over the centuries, especially in the twentieth century. Contemporary theorists criticised the above traditional classification of necessities for a number of reasons, including the following:[16]

1. The scope of traditional *maqāṣid* is the entire Islamic law. However, they fall short to include specific purposes for single scripture/rulings or groups of scripture that cover certain topics or 'chapters' of Islamic law. For example, the traditional theory outlined above does not answer many of the detailed questions of 'why' mentioned before.
2. Traditional *maqāṣid* are concerned with individuals rather than families, societies, and humans, in general, i.e., the subject of the

traditional Islamic criminal law is an individual's soul, honor, or money, rather than the society's life, the society's honor and dignity, or the society's wealth and economy, respectively.

3. The traditional *maqāṣid* classification did not include the most universal and basic values, such as justice and freedom, in its basic theory of levels of necessities.
4. Traditional *maqāṣid* were deduced from the Islamic legal heritage itself, rather than the original sources/scripture. In traditional accounts of *maqāṣid*, reference is always made to rulings of the Islamic law as decided by various Islamic schools of law, rather than referring to the original islamic scripts (verses of the Qur'an, for example) for bases for *maqāṣid*.

To remedy the above shortcomings, modern scholarship introduced new conceptions and classifications of *al-maqāṣid* by giving consideration to new dimensions. Firstly, considering the scope of rulings they cover, contemporary classifications divide *maqāṣid* into three levels:[17]

1. General *maqāṣid*: These *maqāṣid* are observed throughout the entire body of the Islamic law, such as the necessities and needs mentioned above and newly proposed *maqāṣid*, such as 'justice', 'universality', and 'facilitation.'
2. Specific *maqāṣid*: These *maqāṣid* are observed throughout a certain 'chapter' of the Islamic law such as the welfare of children in family law, preventing criminals in criminal law, and preventing monopoly in financial transactions law.
3. Partial *maqāṣid*: These *maqāṣid* are the 'intents' behind specific scripture or rulings, such as the intent of discovering the truth in seeking a certain number of witnesses in certain court cases, the intent of alleviating difficulty in allowing an ill and fasting person to break his or her fasting, and the intent of feeding the poor in banning Muslims from storing meat during Eid/festival days.

In order to remedy the individuality drawback, the notion of *maqāṣid* has been expanded to include a wider scope of people – the community, nation, or humanity, in general. Ibn Ashur (introduced shortly), for example, gave *maqāṣid* that are concerned with the 'nation' (ummah) priority over *maqāṣid* that are concerned with individuals. Rashid Rida, for a second example, included 'reform' and 'women's rights' in his theory of *maqāṣid*. Yusuf al-Qaradawi, for a third example included 'human dignity and rights' in his theory of *maqāṣid*.

The above expansions of the scope of *maqāṣid* allows them to respond to global issues and concerns, and to evolve from 'wisdoms behind the rulings' to practical plans for reform and renewal. They also put *maqāṣid* and its system of values in the centre of the debates over citizenship, integration, and civil rights for Muslim minorities in non-Muslim-majority societies.

Finally, contemporary scholarship has introduced new universal *maqāṣid* that were directly induced from the scripture, rather than from the body of fiqh literature in the schools of Islamic law. This approach, significantly, allowed *maqāṣid* to overcome the historicity of fiqh edicts and represent the scripture's higher values and principles. Detailed rulings would, then, stem from these universal principles. The following are examples of these new universal *maqāṣid* deduced directly from the Islamic scripts:

(1) Rashid Rida (d.1354 AH/1935 CE) surveyed the Qur'an in order to identify its *maqāṣid*, which included, 'reform of the pillars of faith, and spreading awareness that Islam is the religion of pure natural disposition, reason, knowledge, wisdom, proof, freedom, independence, social, political, and economic reform, and women's rights.'[18]

(2) Al-Tahir ibn Ashur (d.1325 AH/1907 CE) proposed that the universal *maqṣid* of the Islamic law is to maintain 'orderliness, equality, freedom, facilitation, and the preservation of pure natural disposition (*fiṭrah*).'[19] It is to be noted that the purpose of 'freedom' (*ḥurriyyah*), which was proposed by Ibn Ashur and several other contemporary scholars, is different from the purpose of 'freedom' (*ᶜitq*), which was mentioned by jurists.[20] *Al-ᶜitq* is freedom from slavery, not 'freedom' in the contemporary sense. 'Will' (*Mashī'ah*), however, is a

well-known Islamic term that bears a number of similarities with current conceptions of 'freedom' and 'free will.' For example, 'freedom of belief' is expressed in the Qur'an as the 'will to believe or disbelieve.'[21] In terms of terminology, 'freedom' (*al-ḥurriyyah*) is a 'newly-coined' purpose in the literature of the Islamic law. Ibn Ashur interestingly, accredited his usage of the term *ḥurriyyah* to 'literature of the French revolution, which were translated from French to Arabic in the nineteenth century CE,'[22] even though he elaborated on an Islamic perspective on freedom of thought, belief, expression, and action in the *mashī'ah* sense.[23]

(3) Mohammad al-Ghazaly (d.1416 AH/1996 CE) called for 'learning lessons from the previous fourteen centuries of Islamic history,' and therefore, included 'justice and freedom' in *maqaṣid* at the necessities level.[24] Al-Ghazaly's prime contribution to the knowledge of *maqāṣid* was his critique on the literalist tendencies that many of today's scholars have.[25] A careful look at the contributions of Mohammad al-Ghazaly shows that there were underlying '*maqāṣid*' upon which he based his opinions, such as equality and justice, upon which he had based all his famous new opinions in the area of women under the Islamic law and other areas.

(4) Yusuf al-Qaradawi (1345 AH/1926 CE-) also surveyed the Qur'an and concluded the following universal *maqāṣid*: 'Preserving true faith, maintaining human dignity and rights, calling people to worship God, purifying the soul, restoring moral values, building good families, treating women fairly, building a strong Islamic nation, and calling for a cooperative world.'[26] However, al-Qaradawi explains that proposing a theory in universal *maqāṣid* should only happen after developing a level of experience with detailed scripture.[27]

(5) Taha al-Alwani (1354 AH/1935 CE-) also surveyed the Qur'an to identify its 'supreme and prevailing' *maqāṣid*, which are, according to him, 'the oneness of God (*tawḥīd*), purification of the soul (*tazkiyah*), and developing civilisation on earth (*ᶜimrān*).'[28] He is currently writing a separate monograph to elaborate on each of these three *maqāṣid*.[29]

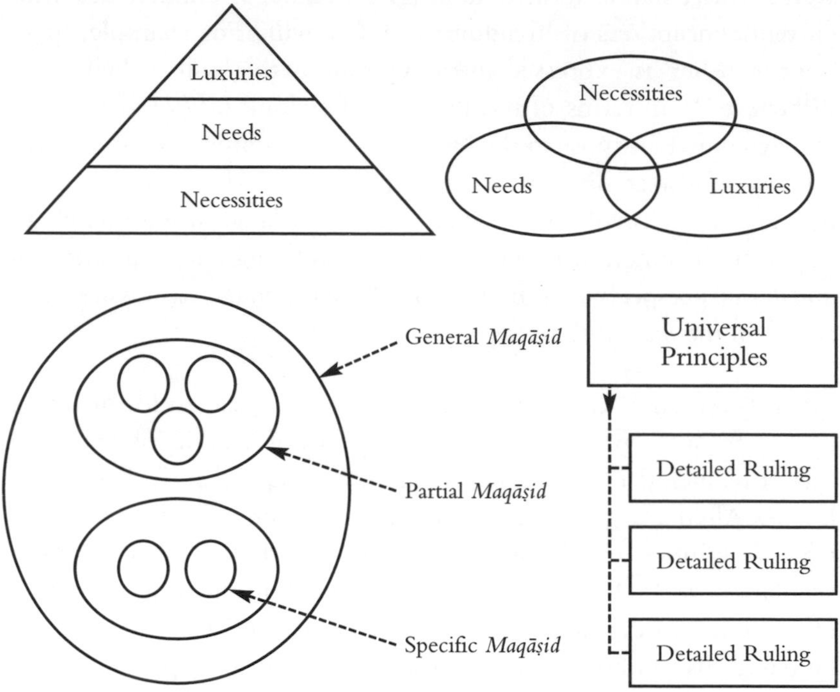

All of the above *maqāṣid* were presented as they appeared in the minds and perceptions of the above jurists. None of the above classic or contemporary classifications and structures could claim to be 'according to the original divine will.' If we refer to nature that God created, we will never find natural structures that could be represented in terms of circles, pyramids, or boxes, as the above diagram shows. All such structures in science and humanities too, and the categories they include, are man-made for the sake of illustration for themselves and other people.

Therefore, *al-maqāṣid* structure is best described as a 'multi-dimensional' structure, in which levels of necessity, scope of rulings, scope of people, and levels of universality are all valid dimensions that represent valid viewpoints and classifications.

The above twentieth-century views also show that *maqāṣid al-sharīʿah* are, actually, representations of each scholar's own viewpoint for reform and development of the Islamic law, despite the fact that all these *maqāṣid* were 'induced' from the scripture. This fusion of the scripture and contemporary needs for reform gives *al-maqāṣid* special significance.

Al-Maqāṣid in the Companions' Ijtihad

The history of the idea of speculating a certain underlying purpose, aim, or intent of Qur'anic or prophetic instructions goes back to the Companions of the Prophet, as narrated in a number of incidents. One clear and popular example is the multi-chained hadith of 'afternoon prayers at Banū Qurayẓah,' in which the Prophet sent a group of Companions to Banū Qurayẓah,[30] and ordered them to pray their afternoon (*ʿaṣr*) prayer there.[31] The span of time allowed for *ʿaṣr* prayers had almost expired before the group reached Banū Qurayẓah. Thus, they found themselves divided into supporters of two different opinions, one opinion entailed praying at Banū Qurayẓah's anyway and the other opinion entailed praying on the way (before the prayer time was over).

The rationale behind the first opinion was that the Prophet's instruction was clear in asking everybody to pray at Banū Qurayẓah, while the rationale of the second opinion was that the Prophet's 'purpose/intent' of the order was to ask the group to hasten to Banū Qurayẓah, rather than 'meaning/intending to' postpone prayers until after its due time. According to the narrator, when the Companions later narrated the story to the Prophet, he approved both opinions.[32] The approval of the Prophet, as jurists and Imams said, entails the permissibility and correctness of both views. The only prime jurist who disagreed with the Companions who prayed on the way was Ibn Ḥazm al-Ẓāhirī (the literalist), who wrote that they should have prayed the 'afternoon prayer' after they reach Banū Qurayẓah, as the Prophet had said, even after midnight![33]

Another incident, which shows a more serious consequence of taking a 'purpose-oriented' approach to the prophetic instructions occurred during the days of ʿUmar, the second caliph. The status of ʿUmar in Islam and his continuous and wide-ranging consultation of a large number of Companions, make his opinions of special significance. In this incident, the Companions asked ʿUmar, to distribute the newly-'conquered' lands of Egypt and Iraq amongst them as some sort of 'spoils of war.' Their argument relied on the clear and specific verses of the Qur'an that allowed fighters their 'spoils of war.'[34] ʿUmar refused to divide whole cities and provinces over the Companions by referring to other verses, with more general expressions, stating that God has a 'purpose' of 'not making the rich dominate wealth.'[35] Therefore, ʿUmar (and the Companions who supported his opinion) understood the specifics of the verses of 'spoils of war' within the context of a certain purpose (*maqṣid*) of the law. This purpose was, 'diminishing the difference between economic levels,' to use familiar contemporary terms.

Another telling example is ʿUmar's application of a moratorium on the (Islamic) punishment for theft during the famine of Madinah.[36] He thought that applying the punishment prescribed in the scripture, while people are in need of basic supplies for their survival, goes against the general principle of justice, which he considered more fundamental.

A third example from ʿUmar's fiqh (application of the law) is when he did not apply the 'apparent meaning' of the hadith that clearly gives a soldier the right to the spoils of war from opponents.[37] He decided to give soldiers only one-fifth of these spoils, if they were 'significantly valuable,' with a purpose to achieve fairness amongst soldiers and enrich the public trust.

A fourth example is ʿUmar's decision to include horses in the types of wealth included in the obligatory charity of zakah, despite the Prophet's clear instruction to exclude them. ʿUmar's rationale was that horses at his time were becoming significantly more valuable than camels, which the Prophet included in zakah at his time.[38] In other words, ʿUmar understood the 'purpose' of the zakah in terms of a form of social assistance that is paid by the wealthy for the sake of the poor, regardless of the exact types of wealth that were mentioned in the prophetic tradition and understood via its literal implication.[39]

All known schools of law, except for the Ḥanafīs, are against such expansion of 'the pool of charity,' which illustrates how literalism had a strong influence on traditional juridical methods. Ibn Ḥazm, again, asserted that, 'there is no zakah on anything except eight types of wealth, which are mentioned in the tradition of the Prophet, namely, gold, silver, wheat, barley, dates, camels, cows, sheep and goats. There is no zakah on horses, commercial goods, or any other type of wealth.'[40] It is clear how such opinion hinders the institution of zakah from achieving any meaningful sense of justice or social welfare.

Based on a 'methodology that considers the wisdoms behind the rulings,' Qaradawi rejected classic opinions on the above matter in his very detailed study on zakah. He wrote: 'Zakah is due on every growing wealth ... The purpose of zakah is to help the poor and to serve the public good. It is unlikely that The Legislator aimed to put this burden on owners of five or more camels (as Ibn Ḥazm had said), and release businessmen who earn in one day what a shepherd earns in years ...'[41]

The above examples are meant to illustrate early conceptions of *maqāṣid* in the application of the Islamic law and the implications of giving them fundamental importance. However this purpose-oriented approach does not simply apply to all rulings of the Islamic law.

Bukhārī narrates that ᶜUmar was asked: 'Why do we still jog around the Kaᶜbah with our shoulders uncovered even after Islam had prevailed in Makkah?' The story behind the question is that after the 'conquest of Makkah,' the people of Makkah claimed the Prophet and his Companions lost their health during their prolonged stay in Madinah. The Prophet therefore ordered the Companions to jog around the Kaᶜbah with their shoulders uncovered in a show of strength. ᶜUmar, however, did not take a purpose-oriented approach to this question. He answered: 'We do not cease doing anything we used to do at the Prophet's time.'[42] ᶜUmar, thus, made a distinction between 'acts of worship' (*ᶜibādāt*) and 'worldly transactions' (*muᶜāmalāt*).

Later Imam al-Shāṭibī for another example, expressed this distinction when he wrote: 'Literal compliance is the default methodology in the area of acts of worship (*ᶜibādāt*), while the consideration of purposes is the default methodology in the area of worldly dealings (*muᶜāmalāt*).'[43] Therefore, generally speaking, the area of 'acts of worship' that is *ᶜibādāt*, should remain a fixed area in which the believer refers to the literal example of the Prophet. However, it is the very example of the Prophet and his Companions not to imitate them, literally, in the various areas of 'transactions' (*muʿāmalāt*) and rather, to go by the principles and '*maqāṣid*.'

Early Theories of Maqāṣid

After the Companions' era, the theory and classifications of *maqāṣid* started to evolve. However, *maqāṣid* as we know them today were not clearly developed until the time of the later *uṣūlīs* of the fifth to eighth Islamic century, as I will elaborate in the next subsection. During the first three centuries, however, the idea of purposes/causes (*ḥikam, ʿilal, munāsabāt,* or *maʿānī*) appeared in a number of reasoning methods utilised by the Imams of the classic schools of Islamic law, such as reasoning by analogy (*qiyās*), juridical preference (*istiḥsān*), and interest (*maṣlaḥah*). Purposes themselves, however, were not subjects of separate monographs or special attention until the end of the third Islamic century. Then, the development of the theory of 'levels of necessity' by Imam al-Juwaynī (d. 478 AH/ 1085 CE) took place much later in the fifth Islamic century. The following is an attempt to trace early conceptions of *al-maqāṣid* between the third and fifth Islamic centuries.

(1) Al-Tirmidhī al-Ḥakīm (d. 296 AH/908 CE). The first known volume dedicated to the topic of *maqāṣid*, in which the term '*maqāṣid*' was used in the book's title, is *al-Ṣalāh wa Maqāṣiduhā* (Prayers and their Purposes) which was written by al-Tirmidhī al-Ḥakīm.[44] The book is a survey of the wisdoms and spiritual 'secrets' behind each of the prayer acts, with an obvious Sufi inclination. Examples are 'confirming humbleness' as the *maqṣid* behind glorifying God with every move during prayers, 'achieving consciousness' as the *maqṣid* behind praising God, 'focusing on one's prayer' as the *maqṣid* behind facing the direction of the Kaʿbah, and so on. Al-Tirmidhī al-Ḥakīm also wrote a similar book on pilgrimage, which he entitled, *al-Hajj wa Asrāruh* (Pilgrimage and its Secrets).[45]

(2) Abū Zayd al-Balkhī (d. 322 AH/933 CE). The first known book on the *maqāṣid* of dealings (that is *muʿāmalāt*) is Abū Zayd al-Balkhī's

al-Ibānah ᶜan ᶜilal al-Diyānah (Revealing Purposes in Religious Practices), in which he surveys purposes behind Islamic juridical rulings. Al-Balkhī also wrote a book dedicated to *maṣlaḥah* which he entitled, *Maṣāliḥ al-Abdān wa al-Anfus* (Benefits for Bodies and Souls), in which he explained how Islamic practices and rulings contribute to health, physically and mentally.[46]

The first page of the Egyptian Dār al-Kutub's manuscript of al-Qaffāl al-Kabīr's 'Maḥāsin al-Sharā'iᶜ' (The Beauties of the Laws).

(3) Al-Qaffāl al-Kabīr Shāshī (d. 365 AH */975* CE*).* The oldest manuscript that I found in the Egyptian Dār al-Kutub on the topic of *al-maqāṣid* is al-Qaffāl's *Maḥāsin al-Sharā'iᶜ* (The Beauties of the Laws).[47] After a 20-page introduction, al-Qaffāl proceeds to divide the book into the familiar chapters of traditional books of fiqh (i.e., starting with purification, and then ablution and prayers, etc.). He mentions each ruling briefly and elaborates on the purposes and wisdoms behind it. The manuscript is fairly clear and contains around 400 pages. The last page mentions the date of the book's completion, which is the 11th of Rabiᶜ 1, 358 AH (7th of February, 969 CE). The coverage of the rulings of fiqh is extensive, albeit strictly addressing individual rulings without introducing any general theory for the purposes. Nevertheless, the book is an important step in the development of *al-maqāṣid* theory. The following is my translation of an excerpt from the introduction (from the first page of the Arabic above):

> ... I decided to write this book to illustrate the beauties of the revealed Law, its magnanimous and moral content, and its compatibility with

> sound reason. I will include in it answers for those who are asking questions about the true reasons and wisdoms behind its rulings. These questions could only come from one of two persons. The first person attributes the creation of the world to its Creator and believes in the truth of prophethood, since the wisdom behind the Law is attributed to the Wise Almighty King, Who prescribes to His servents what is best for them ... The second person is trying to argue against prophethood and the concept of the creation of the world, or maybe is in agreement over the creation of the world while in rejection of prophethood. The logical line that this person is trying to follow is to use the invalidity of the Law as proof for the invalidity of the concept of a Law-Giver...

One part of a different manuscript of al-Qaffāl's *Maḥāsin al-Sharā'iᶜ* was edited and analysed, earlier, by Abd al-Nasir al-Lughani in his Ph.D. thesis written at the University of Wales, Lampeter, in 2004.[48] Mawil Izzi Dien, who supervised this thesis, addressed the significance of the manuscript and al-Shāshī's contribution to the theory of Islamic law. He writes:

> According to Shāshī, the importance of other injunctions is based on their meanings, which are often highlighted by the Legislator. The prohibition of alcohol is an example of this, whereby drink is perceived as a tool with which the devil may create animosity between people, thus preventing them from remembrance of God and prayer ... Shāshī's discussions leaves little doubt that he was providing a further step to his Shāfiᶜī school by establishing a plethora of abstract legal theories to set up reasons for the legal injunctions.[49]

Thus, these 'meanings' and 'reasons,' which al-Qaffāl Shāshī is basing the legal rulings on, represent an early conception of al-*maqāṣid* theory, which was a development in the Shāfiᶜī school. I would add that Shāshī's developments of the concepts of necessities (*ḍarūrāt*), polity (*siyāsah*), or moral actions (*al-makrumāt*) set up the stage for al-Juwaynī and al-Ghazālī's contribution to both the Shāfiᶜī theory and *al-maqāṣid* theory, via further developments of these terms, as explained shortly.

(4) Ibn Bābawayh al-Qummī (d. 381 AH/991 CE). Some researchers claim that research on *maqāṣid al-sharīʿah* was restricted to the Sunni schools of law until the twentieth century.[50] However, the first known monograph dedicated to *maqāṣid* was, in fact, written by Ibn Bābawayh al-Ṣadūq al-Qummī, one of the main Shia jurists of the fourth Islamic century, who wrote a book of 335 chapters on the subject.[51] The book, which was entitled *ʿIlal al-Sharā'iʿ* (The Reasons behind the Rulings), 'rationalises' believing in God, prophets, heaven, and other beliefs. It also gives moral rationales for prayers, fasting, pilgrimage, charity, caring for parents, and other moral obligations.[52]

(5) Al-ʿĀmirī al-Faylasūf (d. 381 AH/991 CE). The earliest known theoretical classification of purposes was introduced by al-ʿĀmirī al-Faylasūf in his *al-Iʿlām bi-Manāqib al-Islām* (Awareness of the Traits of Islam).[53] Al-ʿĀmirī's classification, however, was solely based on 'criminal punishments' in the Islamic law (*ḥudūd*).

Classifications of *maqāṣid* according to 'levels of necessity' were not developed until the fifth Islamic century. Then, the whole theory reached its most mature stage (before the twentieth century CE) in the eighth Islamic century.

(II)
THE 'IMAMS OF *MAQĀṢID*' (FIFTH TO EIGHTH ISLAMIC CENTURIES)

The fifth Islamic century witnessed the birth of what Abdallah Bin Bayyah called 'a philosophy of the Islamic law.'[54] Literal and nominal methods that were developed until the fifth century, proved incapable of coping with the complexities of the evolving civilisation. The theory of 'unrestricted interest' (*al-maṣlaḥah al-mursalah*) was developed as a method that covers 'what was not mentioned in the scripture.' This theory filled a gap in the literal methodologies and, later, gave birth to the theory of *maqāṣid* in Islamic law. The jurists who made the most significant contributions to the *maqāṣid* theory, between the fifth and eighth Islamic centuries are: Abū al-Maᶜālī al-Juwaynī, Abū Ḥāmid al-Ghazālī, al-ᶜIzz ibn ᶜAbd al-Salām, Shihāb al-Dīn al-Qarāfī, Shamsuddīn ibn al-Qayyim and, most significantly, Abū Isḥāq al-Shāṭibī.

Imam al-Juwaynī and 'Public Needs'

Abū al-Maᶜālī al-Juwaynī (d. 478 AH/1085 CE) wrote *al-Burhān fī Uṣūl al-Fiqh* (The Proof in the Fundamentals of Law), which was the first juridical treatise to introduce a theory of 'levels of necessity' in a way that is similar to today's familiar theory. He suggested five levels of *maqāṣid*, necessities (*ḍarūrāt*), public needs (*al-ḥājah al-ᶜāmmah*), moral behavior (*al-makrumāt*), recommendations (*al-mandūbāt*), and 'what cannot be attributed to a specific reason.'[55] He proposed that the purpose of the Islamic law is the protection or inviolability (*al-ᶜiṣmah*) for people's 'faith, souls, minds, private parts, and money.'[56]

Al-Juwaynī's *Ghiyāth al-Umam* (The Salvage of the Nations) was, in my view, another important contribution to *al-maqāṣid* theory, even though it primarily addresses political issues. In that book, al-Juwaynī makes a 'hypothetical assumption' that if jurists and schools of law eventually disappeared from Earth, then, he suggested, the only way to salvage Islam would be to 're-construct' it from the bottom up, using the 'fundamental principles, upon which all rulings of law are based and to which all rulings of law converge.'[57] He wrote that these fundamentals of the law, which he explicitly called '*al-maqāṣid*,' are 'not subject to opposing tendencies and difference of opinion over interpretations.'[58] Examples of these *maqāṣid* upon which al-Juwaynī 'reconstructed' the Islamic law are 'facilitation' in the laws of purification, 'elevating the burden of the poor' in the laws of charity, and 'mutual agreement' in the laws of trade.[59] I view al-Juwaynī's *Ghiyāth al-Umam* as a complete proposal for the 're-construction' of the Islamic law based on *maqāṣid*.

Imam al-Ghazālī and 'Order of Necessities'

Al-Juwaynī's student, Abū Ḥāmid al-Ghazālī (d.505 AH/1111 CE), developed his teacher's theory further in his book, *al-Mustaṣfā* (The

Purified Source). He ordered the 'necessities' that al-Juwaynī had suggested as follows: (1) faith, (2) soul, (3) mind, (4) offspring, and (5) wealth.[60] Al-Ghazālī also coined the term 'preservation' (*al-ḥifẓ*) of these necessities. Despite the detailed analysis that he offered, al-Ghazālī refused to give independent legitimacy (*ḥujjiyyah*) to any of his proposed *maqāṣid* or *maṣāliḥ*, and even called them 'the illusionary interests' (*al-maṣāliḥ al-mawhūmah*).[61] The reason behind this is related to the *maqāṣid* being, sort of, read into the scripture, rather than being implied literally, as other 'clear' Islamic rulings are.

Nevertheless, al-Ghazālī clearly used the *maqṣid* as a basis for a few Islamic rulings. He wrote, for example: 'all intoxicants, whether liquid or solid, are forbidden based on analogy with liquor, since liquor is forbidden for the purpose of the preservation of people's minds.'[62] Al-Ghazālī also suggested a 'fundamental rule,' based on the order of necessities he suggested, which implies that the higher-order necessity should have priority over a lower-order necessity if they generate opposite implications in practical cases.[63]

Al-ʿIzz Ibn ʿAbd al-Salām and 'Wisdoms Behind the Rules'

Al-ʿIzz ibn ʿAbd al-Salām (d.660 AH/1209 CE) wrote two small books about *al-maqāṣid*, in the 'wisdoms-behind-rulings' sense, namely, *Maqāṣid al-Ṣalāh* (Purposes of Prayers) and *Maqāṣid al-Ṣawm* (Purposes of Fasting).[64] However, his significant contribution to the development of the theory of *al-maqāṣid* was his book on interests (*maṣāliḥ*), which he called, *Qawāʿid al-Aḥkām fī Maṣāliḥ al-Anām* (Basic Rules Concerning People's Interests).

Beside his extensive investigation of the concepts of interest and mischief, al-ʿIzz linked the validity of rulings to their purposes and the wisdoms behind them. For example he wrote: 'Every action that misses its purpose is void,'[65] and, 'when you study how the purposes of the law brings good and prevents mischief, you realise that it is unlawful to overlook any common good or support any act of mischief in any situation, even if you have no specific evidence from the script, consensus, or analogy.'[66]

Imam al-Qarāfī and 'Classification of the Prophetic Actions'

Shihāb al-Dīn al-Qarāfī (d.684 AH/1285 CE) contributed to the theory of *maqāṣid*, as we know it today, by differentiating between different actions taken by the Prophet based on the 'intents' of the Prophet himself. He writes in his *al-Furūq* (The Differences):

> There is a difference between the Prophet's actions in the capacity of a conveyer of the divine message, a judge, and a leader ... The implication in the law is that what he says or does as a conveyer goes as a general and permanent ruling ... [However,] decisions related to the military, public trust, ... appointing judges and governors, distributing spoils of war, and signing treaties ... are specific to leaders.[67]

Thus, al-Qarāfī defined a new meaning for '*al-maqāṣid*' as the purposes/intents of the Prophet himself in his actions. Later, Ibn Ashur (d. 1976 CE) developed al-Qarāfi's above 'difference' and included it into his definition of *al-maqāṣid*.[68] Al-Qarāfī also wrote about 'opening the means to achieving good ends,' which is another significant expansion of the theory of *maqāṣid*. He proposed that while means that lead to prohibited ends should be blocked, means that lead to lawful ends should be opened.[69] Thus, he did not restrict himself to the negative side of 'blocking the means' method. More details are presented later.

Imam Ibn al-Qayyim and 'What Shariʿah is all About'

Shamsuddīn ibn al-Qayyim (d. 748 AH/1347 CE) was a student of the renowned Imam Aḥmad ibn Taymiyah (d. 728 AH/1328 CE). Ibn al-Qayyim's contribution to the theory of *maqāṣid* was through a very detailed critique of what is called juridical tricks (*al-ḥiyal al-fiqhiyyah*), based on the fact that they contradict with *maqāṣid*. A trick is a prohibited transaction, such as usury or bribery, which takes an outlook of a legal transaction, such as a sale or a gift, and so on. Ibn al-Qayyim wrote:

> Legal tricks are forbidden acts of mischief because, first, they go against the wisdom of the Legislation and secondly, because they have forbidden

> *maqāṣid*. The person whose intention is usury is committing a sin, even if the outlook of the fake transaction, which he used in the trick, is lawful. That person did not have a sincere intention to carry out the lawful transaction, but rather, the forbidden one. Equally sinful is the person who aims at altering the shares of his inheritors by carrying out a fake sale [to one of them] ... Shariᶜah laws are the cure of our sicknesses because of their realities, not their apparent names and outlooks.

Ibn al-Qayyim summarised his juridical methodology that is based on 'wisdom and people's welfare' with the following strong words:

> The Islamic law is all about wisdom and achieving people's welfare in this life and the afterlife. It is all about justice, mercy, wisdom, and good. Thus, any ruling that replaces justice with injustice, mercy with its opposite, common good with mischief, or wisdom with nonsense, is a ruling that does not belong to the Islamic law, even if it is claimed to be so according to some interpretation.[70]

The above paragraph, in my view, represents a very important 'fundamental rule,' in the light of which the whole Islamic law should be viewed. It places the *maqāṣid* principles in their natural place as 'fundamentals' and a philosophy of the whole law. Imam al-Shāṭibī expressed this view in clearer terms.

Imam al-Shāṭibī and 'Maqāṣid as Fundamentals'

Abū Isḥāq al-Shāṭibī (d. 790 AH/1388 CE). Al-Shāṭibī used, more or less, the same terminology that al-Juwaynī and al-Ghazālī developed. However, I argue that in his *al-Muwāfaqāt fī Uṣūl al-Sharīᶜah* (Congruences in the Fundamentals of the Revealed Law), al-Shāṭibī developed the theory of *al-maqāṣid* in the following three substantial ways:

(i) From 'unrestricted interests' to 'fundamentals of law.' Before al-Shāṭibī's *Muwāfaqāt*, *al-maqāṣid* were included in 'non-restricted interests' and were never considered as fundamentals (*uṣūl*) in their own right, as explained above. Al-Shāṭibī started his volume on *al-maqāṣid* in *al-Muwāfaqāt* by quoting the Qur'an to prove that God has purposes in His creation, sending His messengers, and ordaining laws.[71] Hence, he considered *al-maqāṣid* to be the 'fundamentals of religion, basic rules of the law, and universals of belief' (*uṣūl al-dīn wa qawāᶜid al-sharīᶜah wa kullīyah al-millah*).[72]

(ii) From 'wisdoms behind the ruling' to 'bases for the ruling.' Based on the fundamentality and universality of *al-maqāṣid*, al-Shāṭibī judged that, 'the universals (*al-kulliyyah*) of necessities, needs, and luxuries cannot be overridden by partial rulings (*al-juz'iyyāt*).'[73] This is quite a deviation from traditional fundamentals, even in al-Shāṭibī's Mālikī school, which always gave precendence to 'specific' partial evidences over 'general' or universal evidences.[74] Al-Shāṭibī also made 'knowledge of *maqāṣid*' a necessary condition for the correctness of juridical reasoning (ijtihad) on all levels.[75]

(iii) From 'uncertainty' (*ẓanniyyah*) to 'certainty' (*qaṭᶜiyyah*). In order to support the new status that he gave to *al-maqāṣid* amongst the fundamentals, al-Shāṭibī started his volume on *maqāṣid* by arguing for the 'certainty' (*qaṭᶜiyyah*) of the inductive process that he used to conclude *al-maqāṣid*, based on the high number of evidences he considered,[76] which is also a deviation from the popular 'Greek-philosophy-based' arguments against the validity and 'certainty' of inductive methods. Al-Shāṭibī's book became the standard textbook on *maqāṣid al-sharīᶜah* in Islamic scholarship until the twentieth century but his proposal to present *maqāṣid* as 'fundamentals of the shariᶜah,' as the title of his book suggests, was not as widely accepted.

(III)

MAQĀṢID FOR CURRENT ISLAMIC RENEWAL

Maqāṣid is one of today's most important intellectual means and methodologies for Islamic reform and renewal. Popular media and literature highlight many proposals for reform in the Islamic law and also for the 'integration' of Muslim minorities in their societies, However, these proposals often take, to say the least, a non-friendly approach towards Islam and Muslims, and attempt to 'assimilate' Islam itself and Muslims into certain intellectual and social systems that are alien to them. *Maqāṣid al-sharīʿah* could play a positive role in these debates. It is a methodology from 'within' the Islamic scholarship that addresses the Islamic mind and Islamic concerns. The following sections explain this topic from various points of view.

First, current research in *maqāṣid* is introduced as a project for 'development' and 'human rights,' in the contemporary sense. Secondly, *maqāṣid* is introduced as basis for new opinions in the Islamic law. Thus, the important idea of 'differentiating between means and ends' is explained next. Then, the importance of *maqāṣid* for the re-interpretation of the Qur'an and prophetic traditions is illustrated. The juridical method of 'opening the means' as an extention of the classic method of 'blocking the means' is introduced. The 'universality' of the Islamic law is explained next, and finally, *maqāṣid* is introduced as common grounds between schools of Islamic law and even amongst different systems of faith.

Maqāṣid as a Project for 'Development' and 'Human Rights'

Contemporary jurists/scholars also developed traditional *maqāṣid* terminology in today's language, despite some jurists' rejection of the idea of 'contemporarisation' of *maqāṣid* terminology.[77] Outlined below are some examples of this.

Traditionally, the 'preservation of offspring' is one of the necessities that Islamic law aimed to achieve. Al-ʿĀmirī had expressed it, in his early attempt to outline a theory of necessary purposes, in terms of 'punishments for breaching decency.'[78] Al-Juwaynī developed al-ʿĀmirī's 'theory of punishments' (*mazājir*) into a 'theory of protection,' as mentioned above. Thus, 'punishment for breaching decency' was expressed by al-Juwaynī as, 'protection for private parts.'[79] It was Abū Ḥāmid al-Ghazālī who coined the term 'preservation of offspring' as a purpose of the Islamic law at the level of necessity.[80] Al-Shāṭibī followed al-Ghazālī's terminology, as explained above.

However, in the twentieth century, writers on *maqāṣid*, significantly, developed 'preservation of offspring' into a family-orientated theory. Ibn Ashur, for example, made 'care for the family' to be a *maqṣid* of the Islamic law, in its own right. In his monograph 'The Social System in Islam,' Ibn Ashur elaborated on family-related purposes and moral values in the Islamic law.[81] Whether we consider Ibn Ashur's contribution to be a sort of re-interpretation of the theory of 'preservation of offspring,' or a replacement of the same theory with a new one, it is clear that Ibn Ashur's contribution had opened the door for contemporary scholars to develop the theory of *maqāṣid* in new ways. The orientation of the new views is neither al-ᶜĀmirī's theory of 'punishment' nor al-Ghazālī's concept of 'preservation,' but rather the concepts of 'value' and 'system,' to use Ibn Ashur's terminology. Nevertheless, some contemporary scholars are against the idea of incorporating new concepts, such as justice and freedom, in *maqāṣid*. They prefer to say that these concepts are implicitly included in the classic theory.[82] I think that 'cautiousness' in developing the *maqāṣid* terminology is uncalled for.

Similarly, the 'preservation of mind,' which until recently was restricted to the purpose of the prohibition of intoxicants in Islam, is currently evolving to include 'propagation of scientific thinking,' 'travelling to seek knowledge,' 'suppressing the herd mentality,' and 'avoiding brain drain.'[83]

Likewise, the 'preservation of honor' and the 'preservation of the soul' were at the level of 'necessities' in al-Ghazālī's and al-Shāṭibī's terms. However, these expressions were also preceded by al-ᶜĀmirī's 'punishment' for 'breaching honor' and al-Juwaynī's 'protection of honor.' Honor (*al-ᶜirḍ*) has been a central concept in the Arabic culture since the pre-Islamic period. Pre-Islamic poetry narrates how ᶜAntarah, the famous pre-Islamic poet, fought the Sons of Damdam for 'defaming his honor.' In the hadith, the Prophet described the 'blood, money, and honor of every Muslim' as a 'sanctuary' (*ḥarām*) that is not to be breached.[84] Recently, however, the expression of 'preservation of honor' is gradually being replaced in the Islamic law literature with 'preservation of human dignity' and even the 'protection of human rights' as a purpose of the Islamic law in its own right.[85]

The compatibility of human rights and Islam is a topic of a heated debate, both in Islamic and international circles.[86] A Universal Islamic

Declaration of Human Rights was announced in 1981 by a large number of scholars who represented various Islamic entities at the United Nations Educational, Scientific and Cultural Organisation (UNESCO). Supported by a number of Islamic scriptures mentioned in its references section, the Islamic Declaration essentially includes the entire list of basic rights that were mentioned in the Universal Declaration of Human Rights (UDHR), such as rights to life, freedom, equality, justice, fair trial, protection against torture, asylum, freedom of belief and speech, free association, education, and freedom of mobility.[87]

However, some members of the United Nations High Commission for Human Rights (UNHCHR) expressed concerns over the Islamic Declaration of human rights because they think that it 'gravely threatens the inter-cultural consensus on which the international human rights instruments were based.'[88] Other members believe that the declaration 'adds new positive dimensions to human rights, since, unlike international instruments, it attributes them to a divine source thereby adding a new moral motivation for complying with them.'[89] A *maqāṣid*-based approach to the issue of human rights supports the latter opinion, while addressing the concerns of the former, especially if *al-maqāṣid* terminology is to be 'contemporarized' and made to play a more 'fundamental' role in juridical reasoning. The topic of human rights and *maqāṣid* requires further research in order to resolve the 'inconsistencies' that some researchers have suggested in terms of the application level.[90]

In the same way, the 'preservation of religion,' in al-Ghazālī's and al-Shāṭibī's terminology, had its roots in al-ᶜĀmirī's 'punishment for giving up true faith.'[91] Recently, however, the same theory for that purpose of the Islamic Law has been re-interpreted to mean a dramatically different concept, which is 'freedom of faiths,' to use Ibn Ashur's words,[92] or 'freedom of belief,' in other contemporary expressions.[93] Presenters of these views often quote the Qur'anic verse, 'No compulsion in matters of religion,'[94] as the fundamental principle, rather than what is popularly called 'punishment for apostasy' (*ḥadd al-riddah*) that used to be mentioned in traditional references in the context of the 'preservation of religion.' Thus, thanks to *maqāṣid al-sharīᶜah*, the misconceived, misapplied, and all-politicized 'apostasy' is being replaced with the original Islamic script-based concept of freedom of religion!

Finally al-Ghazālī's 'preservation of wealth,' along with al-ʿĀmirī's 'punishments for theft' and al-Juwaynī's 'protection of money' had recently witnessed an evolution into familiar socio-economic terminology, such as 'social assistance,' 'economic development,' 'flow of money,' 'wellbeing of society,' and 'diminishing the difference between economic levels.'[95] This development enables utilising *maqāṣid al-sharīʿah* to encourage economic growth, which is much-needed in most countries with a majority of Muslims, and also to offer some 'Islamic alternatives' to investment, which are proving to be popular and successful even in today's major developed countries.

'Human development,' the development concept that the UN Development Reports adopt, is much more comprehensive than economic growth. According to the latest United Nations Development Program (UNDP) reports, most countries with a Muslim majority rank lower than the 'developed' range of the comprehensive Human Development Index (HDI). This index is calculated using more than 200 indexes, including measures for political participation, literacy, enrolment in education, life expectancy, access to clean water, employment, standard of living, and gender equality. Nevertheless, some countries with a majority of Muslims, especially oil-rich Arab states, show 'the worst disparities,' the UN report says, between their levels of national income and measures for gender equality, which includes women's political participation, economic participation, and power over resources.[96]

In addition to Muslim minorities who live in developed countries, a few countries with Muslim majorities were ranked under 'high human development,' such as Brunei, Qatar, and the United Arab Emirates. However, the above groups collectively represent less than one percent of Muslims. The bottom of the HDI list includes Yemen, Nigeria, Mauritania, Djibouti, Gambia, Senegal, Guinea, Ivory Cost, Mali, and Niger (which collectively represent around 10 percent of Muslims).

I suggest 'human development' to be a prime expression of *maṣlaḥah* (public interest) in our time, which *maqāṣid al-sharīʿah* should aim to realise through the Islamic law. Thus, the realisation of this *maqṣid* could be empirically measured via the UN 'human development targets,' according to current scientific standards. Similar to the area of human rights, the area of human development requires more research from a *maqāṣid* perspective. Nevertheless, the evolution of 'purposes of Islamic law' into 'human development' gives 'human development targets' a firm base in the Islamic world, instead of presenting them, according to some 'neo-literalists,' as 'tools of western domination.'[97]

Maqāṣid as Basis for New Ijtihad

In Islamic juridical theory, there is a differentiation between opposition or disagreement (*ta^cāruḍ or ikhtilāf*) and contradiction (*tanāquḍ* or *ta^cānud*) of evidences (verses or narrations).[98] Contradiction is defined as 'a clear logical conclusion of truth and falsehood in the same aspect' (*taqāsum al-ṣidqi wa al-kadhib*).[99]

On the other hand, conflict or disagreement between evidences is defined as an 'apparent contradiction between evidences in the mind of the scholar' (*ta^cāruḍun fī dhihn al-mujtahid*).[100] This means that two seemingly disagreeing (*muta^cāriḍ*) evidences are not necessarily in definite non-resolvable contradiction. It is only the perception of the jurist that they are in non-resolvable contradiction which can occur as a result of some missing part of the narration or, more likely, missing information regarding the evidence's timing, place, circumstances, or other conditions.[101]

However, usually, one of the 'opposing' narrations is rendered inaccurate and rejected or cancelled. This method, which is called 'abrogation' (*al-naskh*) suggests that the later evidence, chronologically speaking, should 'abrogate' the former. This means that when verses disagree, the verse that is revealed last is considered to be an abrogating evidence (*nāsikh*) and others to be abrogated (*mansūkh*). Similarly, when prophetic narrations disagree, the narration that has a later date, if dates are known or could be concluded, should abrogate all other narrations. Therefore, a large number of evidences are cancelled, one way or the other, for no good reason other than that the jurists' failing to understand how they could fit them in a unified perceptual framework. The concept of abrogation itself does not have supporting evidence from the words attributed to the Prophet in traditional collections of hadith.[102] The concept of abrogation always appears within the commentaries given by Companions or other narrators, commenting on what appears to be in disagreement with their own understanding of the related issues. According to traditional exegeses, the principle of abrogation does have evidence from the Qur'an, although the interpretations of the related verses are subject to a difference of opinion.[103]

For example, Abū Hurayrah narrated, according to Bukhārī: 'Bad omens are in women, animals, and houses.'[104] However, (also according to Bukhārī) ᶜĀ'ishah narrated that the Prophet had said: 'People during the Days of Ignorance (*jāhiliyyah*) used to say that bad omens are in women, animals, and houses.'[105] These two 'authentic' narrations are thought to be in contradiction. It is telling that most commentators rejected ᶜĀ'ishah's narration, even though other 'authentic' narrations support it. Moreover, it is obvious that Abū Hurayrah, somehow, missed a part of the complete narration.[106] However Ibn al-ᶜArabī for example commented on ᶜĀ'ishah's rejection of the above hadith as follows: 'This is nonsense (*qawlun sāqiṭ*). This is rejection of a clear and authentic narration that is narrated through trusted narrators!'[107] This example shows the implicit bias in the process of 'resolving contradictions.'

Another revealing example is verse 9:5 of the Qur'an, which has come to be named, 'The Verse of the Sword' (*āyah al-sayf*). It states: 'But when the forbidden months are past, then slay the pagans wherever you find them, and seize them.'[108] The historical context of the verse, in the ninth year of *hijrah*, is that of a war between Muslims and the pagans of Makkah. The thematic context of the verse in chapter nine is also the context of the same war, which the chapter is addressing. However, the verse was taken out of its thematic and historical contexts and claimed to have defined the ruling between Muslims and non-Muslims in every place, time, and circumstance. Hence, it was perceived to be in disagreement with more than two hundred other verses of the Qur'an, all calling for dialogue, freedom of belief, forgiveness, peace, and even patience. Conciliation between these different evidences, somehow, was not an option. To solve the disagreement, based on the method of abrogation, most exegetes concluded that this verse (9:5), which was revealed towards the end of the Prophet's life, abrogated each and every 'contradicting' verse that was revealed before it.

Therefore, the following verses were considered abrogated: 'no compulsion in the religion;' 'forgive them, for God loves those who do good to people;' 'repel evil with that which is best;' 'so patiently persevere;' 'do not argue with the People of the Book except with means that are best;' and '(say:) You have your religion and I have my religion.'[109]

Likewise, a large number of prophetic traditions that legitimise peace treaties and multi-cultural co-existence, to use contemporary terms, were also abrogated. One such tradition is 'The Scroll of Madinah' (*ṣaḥīfah al-madīnah*), in which the Prophet and the Jews of Madinah wrote a 'covenant' that defined the relationship between Muslims and Jews living in Madinah. The scroll stated that 'Muslims and Jews are one nation (ummah), with Muslims having their own religion and Jews having their own religion.'[110] Classic and neo-traditional commentators on the *ṣaḥīfah* render it 'abrogated' based on the Verse of the Sword and other similar verses.[111] Seeing all the above scripture and narrations in terms of the single dimension of peace versus war might imply a contradiction, in which the 'final truth' has to 'belong' to either peace or war. The result will have to be an unreasonable fixed choice between peace and war, for every place, time, and circumstance.

What added to the problem is that the number of cases of abrogation claimed by the students of the Companions (*al-tābiᶜīn*) is higher than the cases claimed by the Companions themselves.[112] After the first Islamic century, one could furthermore notice that jurists from the developing schools of thought began claiming many new cases of abrogation, which were never claimed by by the students of the Companions (*tābiᶜīn*). Thus, abrogation became a method of invalidating opinions or narrations endorsed by rival schools of law. Abū al-Ḥasan al-Karkhī (d. 951 CE), for one example, writes: 'The fundamental rule is: Every Qur'anic verse that is different from the opinion of the jurists in our school is either taken out of context or abrogated.'[113] Therefore, it is not unusual in the *fiqhī* literature, to find a certain ruling to be abrogating (*nāsikh*) according to one school and abrogated (*mansūkh*) according to another. This arbitrary use of the method of abrogation has exacerbated the problem of lack of multi-dimensional interpretations of the evidences. A *maqāṣidī* approach could offer a rational and a constructive solution for the dilemmas of opposing evidences. The following are typical examples from the classic literature. It will be shown that the 'opposition' claimed could be resolved via a consideration of the *maqāṣid*.

(1) There is a large number of opposing evidences related to different ways of performing 'acts of worship' (*ᶜibādāt*), all attributed to the Prophet. These opposing narrations have frequently caused heated debates and rifts within Muslim communities. However, understanding these narrations within a *maqṣid* of magnanimity (*taysīr*) entails that the Prophet did carry out these rituals in various ways, suggesting flexibility and tolerance in such matters.[114] Examples of these acts of worship are the different ways of standing and moving during prayers,[115] concluding prayers (*tashahhud*),[116] compensating prostration (*sujūd al-sahū*),[117] reciting 'God is Great' (*takbīr*) during *ᶜĪd* prayers,[118] making up for breaking one's fasting in Ramadan,[119] details of pilgrimage, and so on.

(2) There are a number of opposing narrations that address matters related to customs, that is *al-ᶜurf*, which were also classified as 'in opposition.' However, these narrations could all be interpreted through the *maqṣid* of 'universality of the law.'[120] In other words, differences between these narrations should be understood as differences in the customs for which the various narrations attempted to show consideration, rather than 'contradiction.' One example is the two narrations, both attributed to ᶜĀ'ishah, one of which forbids 'any woman' from marriage without the consent of her guardian, while the other allows previously married women to make their own independent choices on marriage.[121] It is also narrated that ᶜĀ'ishah, the narrator of the two narrations, herself did not apply the 'condition' of consent in some cases.[122] Ḥanafīs explained that, 'the (Arabic) custom goes that a woman who marries without her guardian's consent is

shameless.'[123] Understanding both narrations in the context of considering customs based on the law's 'universality' resolves the contradiction and provides flexibility in carrying out marriage ceremonies according to different customs in different places and times. This approach allows Muslims everywhere to embrace, if they wish, the 'normal' traditions of their societies in such ceremonial areas, and contributes to a culture of tolerance and understanding in multicultural societies.

(3) A number of narrations were classified under cases of abrogation, even though they were, according to some jurists, cases of gradual application of rulings. The purpose behind the gradual applications of rulings on a large scale is, 'facilitating the change that the law is bringing to society's deep-rooted habits.'[124] Thus, 'opposing narrations' regarding the prohibition of liquor and usury, and the performance of prayers and fasting, should be understood in terms of the prophetic 'tradition' of gradual application of high ideals in any given society and, especially, in the case of new Muslims who should slowly grow into their practice of Islam and its teachings.

(4) A number of opposing narrations are considered 'contradictory' because their statements entail different rulings for similar cases. However, taking into account that these prophetic statements addressed different people (Companions) could 'resolve the opposition.' In these cases, the juridical *maqṣid* of 'fulfilling the best interest of people' would be the key to interpreting these narrations based on the differences between these Companions. For example, a few narrations reported that the Prophet told a divorcee that she loses her custody of her children if she gets married.[125] Yet, a number of other 'opposing' narrations entail that divorcees could keep their children in their custody after they get married. The opposing narrations included Umm Salamah's case; Umm Salamah kept custody of her children after she married the Prophet.[126] Thus, relying on the first group of narrations, most schools of law concluded that custody is automatically transferred to the father if the mother gets married. They based their elimination of the second group of narrations on

the fact that the first group was 'more authentic,' being narrated by Bukhārī and Ibn Ḥanbal.[127] Ibn Ḥazm, on the other hand, accepted the second group of narrations and rejected the first group based on his suspicion of one of the narrator's capability of memorisation.[128] However, after citing both opinions, al-Ṣanaʿānī commented: 'The children should stay with the parent who fulfills their best interest. If the mother is the better caregiver and will follow up on the children diligently, then she should have priority over them... The children have to be in the custody of the more capable parent, and the Law cannot possibly judge otherwise.'[129] Thus, fairness is the criteria here and the Law cannot possibly be 'unfair'! This approach allows Muslims to appreciate any fair law-of-the-land that is trying to achieve a sense of justice in the society, even if it were coming from a 'non-Islamic' philosophy or theory.

Differentiating between Means and Ends

Mohammad al-Ghazaly differentiated between 'means' (*al-wasā'il*) and 'ends' (*al-ahdāf*). He allowed the 'expiry' (*intihā'*) of the former and not the latter. Al-Ghazaly mentioned the system of spoils of war, despite the fact that it is mentioned explicitly in the Qur'an, as an example of these 'changeable means.'[130] Recently, Yusuf al-Qaradawi and Faisal Mawlawi, elaborated on the importance of the 'differentiation between means and ends' during the deliberations of the European Council for Fatwa and Research. They, both, applied the same concept to the visual citation of the *hilāl* (Ramadan new moon) being mere means for knowing the start of the month rather than an end in its own right. Hence, they concluded that pure calculations shall be today's means of defining the start and the end of the month of Ramadan, which is a fatwa that solves a number of practical problems for Muslim minorities.[131] Yusuf al-Qaradawi had applied the same concept to Muslim women's garment (*jilbāb*), amongst other things, which he viewed as mere means for achieving the objective of modesty.[132]

In my view, 'differentiating between means and ends' opens a whole lot of possibilities for radically new opinions in the Islamic law. For example, Taha al-Alwani proposed a 'project for reform' in his *Issues in Contemporary Islamic Thought*, in which he elaborated on his version of the method of 'differentiation between means and ends.' The following illustrates how al-Alwani applied this approach to the highly important issue of gender equality.

> The Qur'an transported the people of those times to the realm of faith in absolute gender equality. This single article of faith, perhaps more than any other, represented a revolution no less significant than Islam's condemnation of idolatry...In the case of early Muslim society, given the long established customs, attitudes and mores of pre-Islamic Arabia, it was necessary to implement such changes in stages and to make allowances for society's capacity to adjust itself accordingly ... By establishing a role for a woman in the witnessing of transactions, even though at the time of revelation they had little to do with such matters, the Qur'an seeks to give concrete form to the idea of woman as participant ... The objective is to end the traditional perception of women by including them, "among such as are acceptable to you as witness" ... the matter of witnessing served merely as a means to an end or as a practical way of establishing the concept of gender equality. In their interpretations of "mistake" and "remind," Qur'anic commentators have approached the issue from a perspective based on the assumption that the division of testimony for women into halves is somehow connected with women's inherent inequality to men. This idea has been shared by classical and modern commentators alike, so that generations of Muslims, guided only by *taqlīd* (imitation), have continued to perpetuate this faulty understanding. Certainly, the attitudes engendered by such a misunderstanding have spread far beyond the legal sphere ...[133]

A similar expression is that of Ayatullah Mahdi Shamsuddin's recommendation for today's jurists to take a 'dynamic' approach to the scripture, and 'not to look at every script as absolute and universal legislation, open their minds to the possibility of "relative" legislation for specific circumstances, and not to judge narrations with missing contexts as absolute in the dimensions of time, space, situations, and people.'[134] He further clarifies that he is 'inclined to this understanding but would not base (any rulings) on it for the time being.' Nevertheless he stresses the need for this approach for rulings related to women, financial matters, and to jihad.[135] Fathi Osman, for another example, 'considered the practical considerations' that rendered a woman's testimony to be less than a man's, as mentioned in verse 2:282. Thus, Osman 're-interpreted' the verse to be a function to these practical considerations, in a way similar to al-Alwani's way mentioned above.[136] Hassan al-Turabi holds the same view regarding many rulings related, again, to women and their daily-life practices and 'attires'.[137]

Roger Garaudy's expression of this approach was to 'divide the scripture into a section that could be historicised,' such as, yet again, 'rulings related to women,' and another section that 'represents the eternal value in the revealed message.'[138] Similarly, Abdul-Karim Soroush suggested that the scripture should be 'divided into two parts, essentials and accidentals, accidentals being functions of the cultural, social, and historical environment of the delivery of the main message.'[139] Other similar views regarding the prophetic traditions included Mohammad Shahrour's, who argued that some prophetic traditions in the transactional law are 'not to be considered Islamic law, but rather a civil law, subject to social circumstances, that the Prophet practiced organising society in the area of permissibility, in order to build the Arabic State and Arabic society of the seventh century,' and thus, 'could never be eternal, even if it were true one hundred percent and authentic one hundred percent.'[140]

It is important to note here that some researchers and writers extend the above consideration of historical conditions into what is called the 'historicisation' of Islamic scripture, which is the abrogation or cancellation of their 'authority' in toto. This 'historicist' approach suggests that our ideas about texts, cultures and events are totally a function of their position in their original historical context as well as their later historical developments.[141] Applying this idea, borrowed from literature studies, to the Qur'an entails that the Qur'anic script is a 'cultural product' of the culture that produced it, as claimed by some writers.[142]

Therefore, it is claimed, the Qur'an would become a 'historic document' that is only helpful in learning about a specific historic community that existed in the prophetic era.[143] Haida Moghissi, further, claims that 'the shariʿah is not compatible with the principle of equality of human beings.'[144] For her, 'no amount of twisting and bending can reconcile the Qur'anic injunctions and instructions about women's rights and obligations with the idea of gender equality.'[145] Similarly, Ibn Warraq claims that the Islamic human rights scheme shows 'inadequate support for the principle of freedom.'[146] Thus, according to Moosa, Islamic jurisprudence could not be evidence for an 'ethical vision,' in the contemporary sense.[147]

However, I think that rendering the Qur'an 'unfair' and 'immoral' goes against the very belief in its divine source. Having said that, I also believe that historical events and specific juridical rulings detailed in the Qur'an, should be understood within the cultural, geographical, and historical context of the message of Islam. The key for this understanding is, again, to differentiate between changeable means and fixed principles and ends. Means could 'expire,' as Mohammad al-Ghazaly had put it, while ends and principles are non-changeable. Based on such multi-dimensional understanding, Qur'anic specifics could very well apply universally in every place and time and could very well present an 'ethical vision' for today.

Maqāṣid and Thematic Interpretation of the Qur'an

The 'thematic exegesis school' took steps towards a more purposeful, or *maqāṣidī*, Qur'anic exegesis. The method of reading the Qur'anic text in terms of themes, principles, and higher values, is based on a perception of the Qur'an as a 'unified whole.'[148] Based on this holistic approach, the small number of verses related to rulings, which are traditionally called the 'verses of the rulings' (*āyāt al-aḥkām*), will extend from a few hundred verses to the entire text of the Qur'an. Chapters and verses addressing faith, prophets' stories, the hereafter, and nature will all comprise parts of a holistic picture and, thus, play a role in shaping Islamic juridical rulings. This approach will also allow principles and moral values, which are the main themes behind the Qur'anic stories and sections on the hereafter, to become juridical basis for the rulings, in addition to the literal traditional methods.

A purpose-oriented approach to the narrations of hadith proceeds from a similar holistic and *maqāṣidī* perception of the Prophet's life and sayings. Thus, the authenticity of individual narrations that are incoherent with obvious Islamic values and principles would be put into question. If jurists are not able to reconcile the (linguistic) implication of the two narrations, the authentication of one or another of prophetic narrations is 'based on how much they agree with the principles of the Qur'an.'[149] Thus 'systematic coherence' should be added to the conditions of authenticating the content (*matn*) of these narrations. Finally, a *maqāṣid*-based approach could fill a crucial gap in the narration of hadith, in general, which is the gap of missing contexts. The vast majority of prophetic narrations, in all schools, are composed of one or two sentences or the answer of one or two questions, without elaborating on the historical, political, social, economic, or environmental context of the narration. In some cases the Companion or narrator ends his/her narration by saying: 'I am not sure whether or not the Prophet said ... because (we were in the context) of ....' Usually, however, the context and its impact on how the narration is understood and applied are left to the speculation of the narrator or jurist. A 'holistic picture' helps in overcoming this lack of information through understanding the general purposes of the law.

Interpretation of the Prophetic Intents

In addition to the above, *al-maqāṣid* or the 'intents' of the Prophet, could also be utilised in contextualising narrations. It was explained how al-Qarāfī differentiated between the Prophet's actions 'as a conveyer of the divine message, a judge, and a leader,' and suggested that each of these intents has a different 'implication in the law.' Ibn Ashur added other types of 'prophetic intents,' which is a significant expansion of al-Qarāfī's work, and demonstrated the prophetic intents that he proposed via a number of hadith narrations.[150] The following are some examples, according to Ibn Ashur.[151]

1. The intent of legislation. One example is the Prophet's sermon at the farewell pilgrimage, during which he, reportedly, said: 'Learn your rituals from me [by seeing me performing them], for I do not

know whether I will be performing pilgrimage after this pilgrimage of mine.' He also said after concluding the same sermon: 'Let those present inform those who are absent.' This type of prophetic tradition should be followed exactly.

2. The intent of issuing edicts/fatwa. One example is the Prophet's edicts during his 'farewell pilgrimage,' when a man came to him and said: 'I sacrificed before throwing the pebbles.' The Prophet advised: 'Throw, and don't worry.' Then another man came and said: 'I shaved before sacrificing,' and the Prophet answered: 'Sacrifice, and don't worry.' The narrator said that he was not asked about anything that one would do after or before without his saying, 'Do it, and don't worry.' This type of prophetic tradition should also be followed exactly, in addition to learning certain methods of issuing edicts from them. In the example above, we learn that the order of details of pilgrimage rites, in general, is not a necessary condition for their correctness.
3. The intent of judgeship. Examples are: (1) the Prophet's settlement of the dispute between a man from Hadramawt and a man from Kindah regarding a piece of land; (2) the Prophet's settlement between the Bedouin and his adversary, when the Bedouin said: 'O Messenger of God, judge between us;' and (3) the Prophet's settlement between Ḥabībah and Thābit. Ḥabībah bint Sahl, Thābit's wife, complained to the Prophet that she did not love her husband and that she wanted to divorce him. The Prophet said: 'Will you give him back his walled garden?' She said: 'I have all that he has given to me.' Then, the Prophet said to Thābit: 'Take it from her.' And so he took his walled garden and divorced her. This type of prophetic tradition is not general legislation, as al-Qarāfī had said, and the related verdicts should be up to the judge according to each case.
4. The intent of leadership. Examples are the permission to own barren lands that one cultivates, the prohibition of eating donkey meat in the battle of Khaybar, and the Prophet's statement at the battle of Ḥunayn: 'Whoever has killed an enemy and has evidence of his actions can claim the enemy's property.' In general, the traditions that are related to the socio-eco-political realm

should be understood in terms of their higher purposes of serving public interests.

5. The intent of guidance (which is more general than that of legislation). An example is found in Ibn Suwayd's narration, in which he said: 'I met Abū Dharr, who was wearing a cloak, and his slave, too, was wearing a similar one. I asked the reason for it. He replied, "I scolded a slave by calling his mother bad names. The Prophet said to me, 'O Abū Dharr! Did you abuse him by calling his mother bad names? You still have some characteristics of the age of pagan ignorance. Your slaves are your brethren.'"' In this example, the prophetic guidance was leading the Companions towards freeing slaves. Jurists frequently said: The Legislator aims to accomplish freedom (*al-shāri*ᶜ *mutashawwiq li al-ḥurriyyah*).
6. The intent of conciliation. One example is when the Prophet requested Barīrah to return to her husband after she divorced him. Barīrah said: 'O God's Apostle! Do you order me to do so?' He said, 'No, I only intercede for him.' She said, 'I do not need him.' Also, Bukhārī reported that when Jābir's father died, Jābir asked the Prophet to speak with his father's creditors so that they might waive some of his debt. The Prophet then accepted their refusal to do so. Another example of conciliation is when Kaᶜab ibn Mālik demanded repayment of a debt from ᶜAbdullāh ibn Abū Ḥadrad, the Prophet requested Kaᶜab to deduct half of the debt, and Kaᶜab agreed. In these cases, the Companions understood that the Prophet did not mean to place any obligation on them.
7. The intent of giving advice. One example is when ᶜUmar ibn al-Khaṭṭāb gave someone a horse as charity and the man neglected it. ᶜUmar wished to buy the horse from the man, thinking that he would sell it cheaply. When he asked the Prophet about it, he told him: 'Do not buy it, even if he gives it to you for one dirham, for someone who takes back his charity is like a dog swallowing its own vomit.' Also, Zayd narrated that the Prophet said: 'Do not sell the fruits before their benefit is evident,' but Zayd commented that this was, 'only by way of advice, for some people had quarreled too much over that matter.' In these cases, as well, the Companions understood that the Prophet did not mean to place any obligation on them.

8. The intent of counseling. For example Bashīr informed the Prophet that he had given one of his sons a special gift. The Prophet asked him: 'Have you done the same with all your sons?' He said: 'No.' The Prophet said: 'Do not call me as a witness to injustice.' Also, in these cases, the Companions understood that the Prophet did not mean to place any obligation on them.
9. The intent of teaching high ideals. For example, the Prophet asked Abū Dharr: 'Do you see (the mountain of) Uḥud?' Abū Dharr replied: 'I do!' The Prophet said: 'If I had gold equal to the mountain of Uḥud, I would love that, before three days had passed, not a single Dinar thereof remained with me if I found somebody to accept it, excluding some amount that I would keep for the payment of my debts.' Similarly, al-Barā' ibn ᶜĀzib said: 'God's Messenger commanded us to practice seven things and prohibited us from practicing seven. He commanded us to visit the sick, to walk behind funeral processions, to pray for someone upon sneezing, to approve of someone's oath, to help the oppressed person, to spread the greeting of peace, and to accept the invitation of the invitee. On the other hand, he prohibited us from wearing gold rings, using silver utensils, using red saddlecloth made of cotton, wearing Egyptian clothes with silky extensions, clothes made of thick silk, thin silk, or normal silk.' Similarly, ᶜAlī ibn Abī Ṭālib narrates: 'God's Apostle forbade me to use gold rings, to wear silk clothes and clothes dyed with saffron, and to recite the Qur'an while bowing and prostrating in prayer. I am not saying that he forbade you these things.' Likewise, with the same educational intent, the Prophet told Rafiᶜ ibn Khadīj: 'Do not rent your farm, but cultivate the land yourself.' Also, in these cases, the Companions understood that the Prophet did not mean to place any obligation on them.
10. The intent of disciplining his Companions. For example, the hadith: 'By God! He does not believe! By God! He does not believe!' It was said, 'Who is that, O Messenger of God?' He said: 'The person whose neighbor does not feel safe from his evil.'
11. Intent of non-instruction. This includes the hadith that described the way the Prophet ate, wore his clothes, laid down, walked,

mounted his animal, and placed his hands when prostrating in prayer. Another example is the report that the Prophet stopped on the farewell pilgrimage at a hill overlooking a watercourse in Banī Kinānah, on which ᶜĀ'ishah commented: 'Camping at al-Abṭaḥ is not one of the ceremonies of Hajj, but was simply a place where the Prophet used to camp so that it might be easier for him to leave for Madinah.'

Ibn Ashur's 're-interpretation' of the above narrations of hadith raises the level of 'purposefulness' in traditional methods and allows much flexibility in interpreting and applying the scripture.

'Opening the Means' in Addition to 'Blocking the Means'

Blocking the means (*sadd al-dharā'i*ᶜ) in the Islamic law entails forbidding, or blocking, a lawful action because it could be means that lead to unlawful actions.[152] Jurists from various schools of Islamic law agreed that in such case 'leading to unlawful actions' should be 'more probable than not,' but they differed over how to systemise the comparison of probabilities. Jurists divided 'probability' of unlawful actions into four different levels.[153]

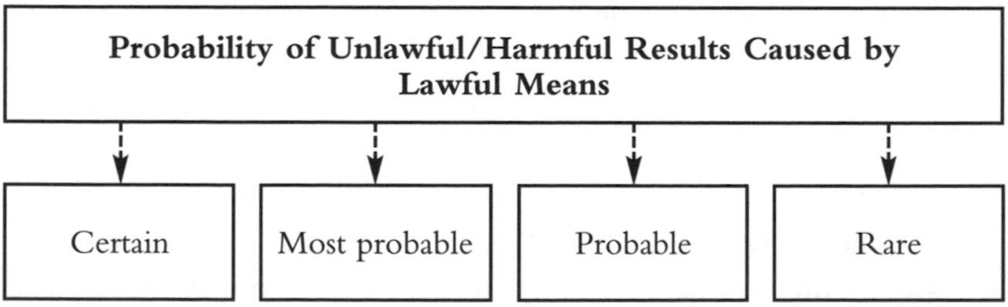

Four 'categories' of probability, according to jurists who endorsed blocking the means, namely, certain, most probable, probable, and rare.

The following are examples that jurists mentioned to illustrate the above categories:

1. A classic example of an action that results in a 'certain' harm is 'digging a well on a public road,' which will certainly harm people. Jurists agreed to block the means in such case, but had a difference of opinion over whether the well-digger, in this example, would be liable for any harm that would happen to people because of his/her action. The difference of opinion is actually over whether prohibiting some action entails making people liable for the resulting damage if they carry that action out, or not.
2. An example of an action that results in a 'rare' harm, according to al-Shāṭibī, is selling grapes, even though a small number of people will use them to make wine. 'Blocking the means' does not apply to such action, jurists agreed, 'since the benefit of the action is more than the harm, which happens in rare cases in any case.'[154]
3. Harm is 'most probable,' jurists argued, when 'weapons are sold during civil unrest or grapes are sold to a wine-maker.'[155] The schools of Mālikīs and Ḥanbalīs agreed to block these means, while others disagreed because, as they argued, harm has to be 'certain' to justify blocking its means.
4. Harm is 'probable' some jurists claimed, 'when a woman travels by herself,' and 'when people use legally-correct contracts with hidden tricks as means to usury.'[156] Again, Mālikīs and Ḥanbalīs agreed to block these means, while others disagreed because the harm is not 'certain' or 'most probable.'

The above classic examples show that, again, 'means' and 'ends' are subject to variations in economic, political, social, and environmental circumstances, and not constant rules. 'A woman travelling by herself,' 'the selling of weapons,' or 'selling of grapes' could lead to probable harm in some situations, but could definitely be harmless or even beneficial for people in other situations. Therefore, it is inaccurate to classify actions according to probabilities of harm in 'hard' categories, as shown above.

Ethically speaking, 'blocking the means' is a consequentialist approach.[157] It could be useful in some situations, but could also be misused by some pessimistic jurists or politically-motivated authorities. Today, 'blocking the means' is a recurring theme in current neo-literalist approaches, which is utilised by some authoritarian regimes for their own ends, especially in the areas of laws related to women. For example, in the name of blocking the means, women are prohibited from 'driving cars,' 'travelling alone,' 'working in radio or television stations,' 'serving as representatives,' and even 'walking in the middle of the road.'[158] To illustrate one such misapplication of 'blocking the means,' the following is a fatwa, which I find rather amusing! It was issued by the Saudi High Council of Fatwa regarding women driving cars.[159]

[Question]: Under circumstances of necessity, is it permissible for a woman to drive an automobile by herself, without the presence of a legal guardian, instead of riding in a car with a non-maḥram man [stranger]?
[Fatwa]: It is impermissible for a woman to drive an automobile, for that will entail unveiling her face or part of it. Additionally, if her automobile were to break down on the road, if she were in an accident, or if she were issued a traffic violation she would be forced to co-mingle with men. Furthermore, driving would enable a woman to travel far from her home and away from the supervision of her legal guardian. Women are weak and prone to succumb to their emotions and to immoral inclinations. If they are allowed to drive, then they will be freed from appropriate oversight, supervision, and from the authority of the men of their households. Also, to receive driving privileges, they would have to apply for a license and get their picture taken. Photographing women, even in this situation, is prohibited because it entails *fitnah* [mischief] and great perils!!

Some Mālikīs proposed 'opening the means' (*fatḥ al-dharā'iᶜ*) in addition to 'blocking' them (*sadd al-dharā'iᶜ*).[160] Al-Qarāfī divided rulings into means (*wasā'il*) and ends/purposes (*maqāṣid*) and suggested that means that lead to prohibited ends should be blocked, and means that lead to lawful ends should be opened.[161] Thus, al-Qarāfī linked the ranking of means to the ranking of their ends, and suggested three levels for ends, namely, 'most repugnant' (*aqbaḥ*), best (*afḍal*), and 'in between' (*mutawassiṭah*). Ibn Farḥūn (d. 769 AH), also from the Mālikī school, applied al-Qarāfī's 'opening the means' to a number of rulings.[162]

Most repugnant ends: Forbidden means	Ends 'in between': Lawful means	Best ends: Obligatory means

Levels of ends and alternative levels of means, according to al-Qarāfī.

Thus Mālikīs do not restrict themselves to the 'negative side of consequentialist ethics,' to borrow a term from moral philosophy. They expand this method of thinking to the positive side of it, which entails opening means to achieving good ends even if these ends were not mentioned in specific scripture. And in order to give al-Qarāfi's *maqāṣid*-based expansion of blocking the means more flexibility, the following chart suggests a 'continuous' measure of 'goodness' and 'repugnance' of ends, to use al-Qarāfī's expressions. 'Neutral' ends, then, would entail 'lawful' means.

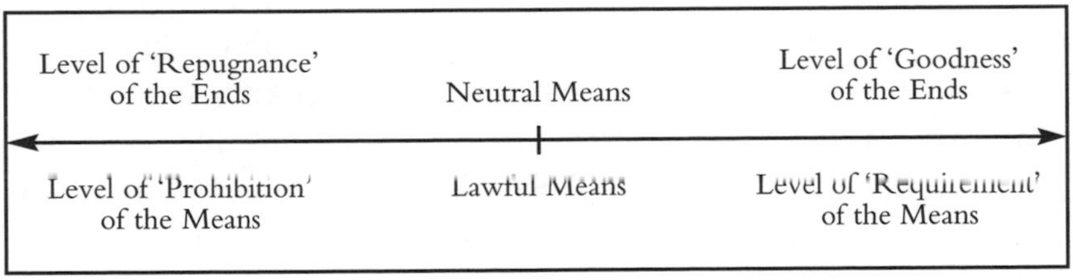

A spectrum of levels between good ends/required means and repugnant ends/ prohibited means.

Achieving the 'Universality' Maqṣid

Al-ʿUrf literally means custom or, more accurately, a 'good' custom that the community approves.[163] In the *First Encyclopaedia of Islam*, Levy confirms his conceptual separation between *ʿurf* and *sharʿ*. He writes:

> ʿURF (A.), defined by Djurdjani (Taʿrifat, ed. Flügel, p.154) as "[Action or belief] in which persons persist with the concurrence of the reasoning powers and which their natural dispositions agree to accept [as right]". It stands therefore to represent unwritten custom as opposed to established law, *sharʿ* though attempts have not been lacking to regard it as one of the *uṣūl.*

However, the relationship between the Islamic law (*sharʿ*) and *ʿurf* is far more complex than the above dichotomy. Arabic *ʿurf*, especially during the early era of Islam, had indeed influenced a number of *fiqhī* provisions. Al-Tahir ibn Ashur proposed a novel view of the fundamental of 'custom' (*al-ʿurf*) based on the purposes of Islamic law. He wrote a chapter in his '*Maqāṣid al-Sharīʿah*' on *al-ʿurf* which was entitled with a *maqṣid* that he called, 'The Universality of the Islamic Law.'[164] In this chapter, he did not consider the effect of custom on the application of narrations, as is the traditional view. Instead, he considered the effect of (Arabic) customs on narrations themselves. The following is a summary of Ibn Ashur's argument.

First, Ibn Ashur explained that it is necessary for the Islamic law to be a universal law, since it claims to be 'applicable to all humankind everywhere on earth at all times,' as per a number of Qur'anic verses and hadith that he cited.[165] Then, Ibn Ashur elaborated on the wisdoms behind choosing the Prophet from amongst Arabs, such as the Arabs' isolation from civilisation, which prepared them, 'to mix and associate openly with other nations with whom they had no hostilities, in contrast to Persians, Byzantines, and Copts.' Yet, for the Islamic law to be universal, 'its rules and commands should apply equally to all human beings as much as possible,' as Ibn Ashur confirmed. That is why, he wrote, 'God had based the Islamic law on wisdoms and reasons that can be perceived by the mind and which do not change according to nations and custom.' Thus, Ibn Ashur provided explanation as to why the Prophet forbade his Companions to write down what he said, 'lest particular cases be taken as universal rules.' Ibn Ashur began applying his ideas to a number of narrations, in an attempt to filter out Arabic customs from popular traditional rulings. He wrote:[166]

> Therefore, Islamic law does not concern itself with determining what kind of dress, house, or mount people should use ... Accordingly, we can establish that the customs and mores of a particular people have no right, as such, to be imposed on other people as legislation, not even the people who originated them ... This method of interpretation has removed much confusion that faced scholars in understanding the reasons why the law prohibited certain practices ... such as the prohibition for women to add hair extensions, to cleave their teeth, or to tattoo themselves ... The correct meaning of this, in my view ... is that these practices mentioned in hadith were, according to Arabs, signs of a woman's lack of chastity. Therefore, prohibiting these practices was actually aimed at certain evil motives ... Similarly, we read: ... 'believing women should draw over themselves some of their outer garments' (*Surat al-Aḥzāb*) ... This is a legislation that took into consideration an Arab tradition, and therefore does not necessarily apply to women who do not wear this style of dress ...

Therefore, based on the purpose of 'universality' of the Islamic law Ibn Ashur suggested a method of interpreting narrations through understanding their underlying Arabic cultural context, rather than treating them as absolute and unqualified rules. Thus, he read the above narrations in terms of their higher moral purposes, rather than norms in their own right. This approach allows great flexibility in the law and accommodation of local cultures, especially in non-Arabic environments.

Maqāṣid as Common Grounds between Schools of Islamic Law

Today, in the beginning of the twenty-first century, sharp 'scholastic' divisions take place between each pair of schools of Islamic law. The sharpest and most devastating of these divisions is the Sunni-Shia division, which many like to perceive as a 'sectarian' division, for various political motives. The apparent differences of the past and present between various Sunni and Shia schools, as people familiar with Islamic law could assert, boil down to their 'differences over politics' rather than their 'pillars of faith.' However, today, deep divisions between Sunni and Shia are constructed through courts, mosques, and social dealings in most countries, causing these divisions to develop into violent conflict in a number of countries. These divisions have added to a wide-spreading culture of civil intolerance and inability of coexistence with the 'Other.'

I carried out a survey on the latest studies on *al-maqāṣid*, which were written by key Sunni and Shia scholars. The survey revealed to me an interesting identicalness between both approaches to *maqāṣid*.[167] Both approaches address the same topics (ijtihad, *qiyās, ḥuqūq, qiyam, akhlāq,* and so on), refer to the same jurists and books (al-Juwaynī's *Burhān*, Ibn Bābawayh's *ᶜIlal al-Sharā'iᶜ*, al-Ghazālī's *Mustaṣfā*, al-Shāṭibī's *Muwāfaqāt*, al-Sader's *Uṣūl*, and Ibn Ashur's *Maqāṣid*), and use the same theoretical classifications (*maṣāliḥ, ḍarūrāt, ḥājiyyāt, taḥsīniyyat, maqāṣid ᶜāmmah, maqāṣid khāṣṣah*, and so on). Most of the juridical differences between Sunni and Shia *fiqhī* schools are due to differences over a few narrations and a handful of practical rulings.

A *maqāṣidī* approach to fiqh is a holistic approach that does not restrict itself to one narration or view, but rather refers to general principles and common ground. Implementing the 'higher' purposes of unity and reconciliation of Muslims has a higher priority over implementing *fiqhī* details. Accordingly, Ayatullah Mahdi Shamsuddin prohibited aggression along Shia-Sunni lines based on 'the higher and fundamental purposes of reconciliation, unity, and justice.'[168]

A *maqāṣidī* approach takes the issues to a higher philosophical ground and, hence, overcomes differences over the political history of Muslims and encourages a much-needed culture of conciliation and peaceful co-existence.

Maqāṣid as Common Basis for Inter-Faith Dialogue

Systematic theology is an approach to religion or a certain system of faith that attempts to draw an overall picture. It is an approach that considers all aspects related to that religion or faith, such as history, philosophy, science, and ethics, in order to come up with a holistic philosophical view. The approach that bears the name 'systematic theology,' is becoming increasingly popular, especially in Christian theology with all of its denominations.

Christian systematic theology asks the following question: 'what does the whole Bible teach us today about a given topic?'[169] As such, it involves a 'process of collecting and synthesizing all the relevant Scriptural passages for various topics,'[170] such as prayers, justice, righteousness, compassion, mercy, unity, diversity, morality, salvation, and a variety of other themes.[171] Thus systematic theology uses an 'inductive method'[172] that results in the 'grouping, classifying, and integrating' of 'disconnected truths,' even referred to as 'undigested facts' until their interrelations and the underlying 'dogmas'[173] or 'coherent summaries' become evident.[174]

The necessity of a systematic approach to theology is justified by Charles Hodge (1797–1878 CE) based on the following:[175]

1. The constitution of the human mind cannot help endeavoring to systemise and 'reconcile the facts which it admits to be true.'
2. The accumulation of isolated facts results in a much higher kind of knowledge.
3. This process is necessary for a satisfactory exhibition of the truth and 'defending it from objections.'
4. This is the 'nature' of the physical world and the revelation, as defined by God, who 'wills that men should study His works and discover their wonderful organic relation and harmonious combination.'

Systematic theology, in the above sense, bears a lot of obvious practical similarities with the *maqāṣidī* approach to Islam that this book has been illustrating all along. Both approaches deploy the concept of 're-interpretation' to provide bases for dynamism and flexibility to changing worldviews, without compromising the basic references of believers to their Scripture.

The classic theory of *maqāṣid* defines areas of necessities (*ḍarūrāt*) that are meant to be preserved and protected by the Shari'ah, such as 'the preservation of faith, life, wealth, minds, and offspring.'[176]

Similarly, systematic theologians write on similar concepts, such as the importance of protecting life and health, protecting souls by 'prohibiting drunkenness' (even though the Islamic approach is to prohibit all amounts and forms of intoxicants as a form of 'blocking the means' to drunkenness), the necessity of nurturing the family, and so on.[177]

A holistic (*maqāṣidī*) view allows theologians to place specific religious teachings and commands within a general framework of their underlying principles and governing objectives, rather than focusing on a piece-by-piece understanding and, therefore, a literal application of these teachings and commands. Thus, moral values intended by various commands will not be different across the religious spectrum, despite the fact that they take different forms in their specific practical environments.

Hence, I believe that the above purpose-based approach to theology could play a significant role in inter-faith dialogue and also in understanding. It reveals commonalities that are necessary for such dialogue and understanding.

Maqāṣid al-Sharīʿah Applied

Questions and Answers on Ethics

I received the following questions from various people in different countries via islamonline.net, via its readingislam.net 'Ask About Islam' forum, and also via other correspondences by email. I took some liberties in editing these questions and answers, in order to remove the parts that are irrelevant to the topic of this book. The purpose of this section is to illustrate how *maqāṣid al-sharīʿah* could provide answers to some pressing contemporary questions about the Islamic law that are asked by Muslims and non-Muslims everywhere.

[Q]: *The "maqṣid" (intention/goal) of Shariʿah in general is ethics (akhlāq), right? Being a born Muslim who has lived in the West I see a vast gap between the ethical code of Islam and the Western code of ethics. The gap I mean is related to the eternity and solidarity of this code of ethics. I mean that what was considered negative 1400 years ago in Islam is still negative in Islam today, while this is not the case in the Western ethical code. Please give me your reflection on the matter.*

[A]: Well. I will make two points in an attempt to address this serious and important topic: 1) Let us differentiate between ethical values (ideals and *maqaṣid*) and ethical decisions (which are applications of these values in the real world). Ideal *maqāṣid* and values (such as justice, equality, honesty, freedom, modesty, tolerance, etc.) are not supposed to be subject to 'evolution' with the change of places and eras. But ethical norms, which are the practical implications of these ideals, could change in a way that preserves and promotes the original ideals, subject to the changes in place and time. For example, justice is the same in every place and time. But the application of this concept in courts for example, is clearly subject to what the society thinks is 'fair' according to their culture and context. For instance, justice entails certain legal rights, and responsibilities, for each family member given a certain social system. These rights and responsibilities could be different in a different social system, where the roles of family members differ in significant ways. This difference, or 'cultural specifity,' has to be taken into account in order to maintain justice itself.

2) However, there are certain 'acts of worship' (Arabic *ᶜibādāt*) in Islam that are supposed to be taken for granted and are not supposed to be subject to change. These are the common cultural component of Islam, if you wish, that every Muslim should embrace, wherever they are. Clear examples are Muslims' daily five prayers (and the way we pray, the way we wash before the prayer, the number of prayers and their timings, bowing, supplications, etc.) and the annual charity zakah (including its percentages and the groups of people who receive it, etc.). Muslims in these acts of worship are simply following the example of the Last Prophet, Muhammad, and are not supposed, as a general rule, to 'develop' or change them based on some wisdom or rationale behind them that one might conclude. On the other hand, actions that are in the category of 'transactions' (or *muᶜāmalāt*) are supposed to be subject to how much they achieve the wisdoms behind them and the underlying moral rationales.

Also, in my view, forbidding certain actions (such as drinking any amount of alcohol, gambling, usury, and promiscuity) fall under the category of Islamic 'acts of worship' that are stated in clear and non-disputed terms in the Islamic scripture. We could reflect upon the wisdom behind these rules and we could sure discuss whether what I think is a wisdom behind one rule or the other is real or not, and so on. But at the end, there are certain rulings that every Muslim should apply as a sort of practicing of Islam.

[Q]: *How can Islamic laws facilitate ethics to grow in a Muslim society in this rapidly changing modern world?*

[A]: Islamic law has a unique feature which is that it always aims to achieve specific ethical or moral *maqāṣid* by its religiously ordained rules. Islamic rulings of *ᶜibādāt* (acts of worship) and *muᶜāmalāt* (dealings) are all aiming at specific moral objectives. The Prophet was 'sent merely to perfect morals,' he said. For specific examples, God mentioned that regular prayer: "forbids (people) from immoral actions" (29:45), that during Hajj "no immorality and no mischief should take place" (2:197), and that charity is for purifying the rich (from greed) and for helping the poor and needy. Similarly, all the rules that jurists suggested for trade and for contracts, etc., are all aiming to achieve certain values, such as, fairness, honesty, protecting the weak, etc. Islamic laws (correctly applied) do spread morality in society. In other words Islamic law is a 'moral law' rather than 'theocratic law,' to use modern language in general terms.

[Q]: *The Qur'an says that Muhammad is a "mercy to all beings." How is this reflected through the rigid system of Islamic Shariᶜah law? Don't you find contradiction between the rigidity of Shariᶜah and mercy as being the ultimate goal of the existence of Muhammad? Please clarify.*

[A]: Yes. The Prophet Muhammad is "a mercy to all beings" (21:107). But I don't think that there is a problem with "Shariᶜah," which is a moral and merciful Islamic way of life. I often mention the saying of the great Imam Shamsuddīn ibn al-Qayyim (d. 748 AH/ 1347 CE) who said:

Shariʿah is all about wisdom and achieving people's welfare in this life and the afterlife. It is all about justice, mercy, wisdom, and good. Thus, any ruling that replaces justice with injustice, mercy with its opposite, common good with mischief, or wisdom with nonsense, is a ruling that does not belong to the Shariʿah, even if it is claimed to be so according to some interpretation.

However, there are some major problem with some old and new misinterpretations and misapplications of this Shariʿah. So, while Shariʿah is aiming to achieve the objectives or *maqāṣid* of justice, mercy, wisdom, and good, some people in influential political and/or intellectual positions mistakenly use Shariʿah as means for political control. Thus, they publicize a certain understanding of the Shariʿah in order to gain some worldly gains. These people give the Shariʿah a bad name and harm Islam more than its enemies.

[Q]: *Love is an ultimate goal of life and sharing love and finding it with the person who is really suitable is real ultimate happiness. Why can't we be left to enjoy the beauty of peaceful love, with no burdens of a complicated family? How can you regard this prohibition of physical love as being ethical and part of the "ethical goals of Shariʿah"?*

[A]: This is one area in which the practices of many Muslims were simply unfair to the Shariʿah. I agree that love is one of the most beautiful things that God created on this earth, and it is totally human to love someone and, therefore, to want to have a physical relationship with that person to express that love. Islam is not against that. Islam only regulates that! Islam did not forbid love! Islam forbade 'physical intimacy between unmarried couples.' Why? Because Islam is balancing this value of love with another value, which is the welfare of the family, which is the unit of a good society, from the Islamic perspective.

Thus if a married man or woman commits adultery Islam considers this act to be a "crime," because, even though it could be an expression of love, it is against the very core of the ideal family that Islam envisions. On the other hand, if the lovers are unmarried,

Islam does not forbid them to love each other, but it forbids them from expressing this love in a physical way outside marriage. Again, this rule is trying to balance the value of love with family values. On the other hand, Islam encourages marriage and facilitates it in various ways. The Prophet had said: "The best thing that two persons who love each others could do is to get married," (narrated by Imam Aḥmad and others). And what if that physical relationship, I mean between unmarried couples, produces children? Is this fair to these children to come into a relationship without commitment?

I would like to also mention that if the couple choose not to have children for some reason, perhaps because they are too young or because of what you called "burdens of a complicated family," Islam is not against that. But at least, if a child ever arrives, it should arrive within a family. This saves these children from a great deal of injustice, and the current situation of single mothers in various countries proves this point. So, love is a wonderful goal, as you mentioned, but Islam aims to balance it with other social and family goals.

[Q]: *How can Islam be an ethical way of life if it encourages terrorism?*

[A]: I will answer this question by listing what terrorism is NOT and then what terrorism is, so the answer becomes self-explanatory.

• Terrorism is not equal to any religion. It is not fair for Islam, Christianity, Judaism, Hinduism, or Buddhism to be associated with terrorism. The best way to judge a religion is to read its scripture. These religions, according to their scripture, propagate a certain way of viewing The Divine and the world, and train their followers to specific principles of morality and spirituality, albeit in different ways and various expressions.

• Terrorism is not equal to violence either. In fact, according to all rational human beings, some shapes and forms of violence are valid. For example, violence is necessary to defend yourself when somebody attacks you in the street. Violence is needed sometimes to arrest and punish criminals (in this case, it is the government's job to do that). People justifiably use violence to hunt (unless of course they are vegetarian). And so on. Therefore, violence in itself is not a vice. But, the way that it is used in a certain context could make it a vice or a virtue.

• Terrorism does not include self-defense. Imagine for example that some people with arms invaded your area, kicked you out of your own home, and occupied it. Don't you think that you are entitled to self-defense? This self-defence, however, is not supposed to lead you to commit injustices against other innocent people and should be only against those who invaded your home.

• Terrorism is not restricted to individuals. There are terrorist groups, which use organized guerrillas for their goals, and there are terrorist governments, which use armies and weapons of various degrees of destruction against innocent people. People could even be 'terrorized' and harmed via other means, such as hunger, torture, deprivation from medical care, economic sanctions on a large scale, and so on.

• Terrorism is not restricted to non-combat zones. Acts of terrorism could take place in combat zones and war zones if basic war ethics for civilians, soldiers, or captives of war are not respected and observed.

Therefore, an act of terrorism is an act in which innocent civilians or non-civilians are harmed or hurt in a way that goes against the basic concepts and objectives of justice and human rights. The *maqāṣid*-based definition of terrorism is the following: An act of terrorism is an act in which innocent people (civilians or non-civilians) are harmed in any way that goes against the principles of justice and human dignity.

Conclusion

Current applications (or rather, misapplications) of Islamic law are reductionist rather than holistic, literal rather than moral, one-dimensional rather than multidimensional, binary rather than multi-valued, deconstructionist rather than reconstructionist, and causal rather than teleological. There is lack of consideration and functionality of the overall purposes and underlying principles of the Islamic law as a whole. Moreover, exaggerated claims of 'rational certainty' (or else, 'irrationality') and 'consensus of the infallible' (or else, 'historicity of the scripts') add to lack of spirituality, intolerance, violent ideologies, suppressed freedoms, and authoritarian regimes. Thus, a *maqāṣidī* approach takes juridical issues to a higher philosophical ground, and hence, overcomes (historical) differences over politics between Islamic schools of law, and encourages a much-needed culture of conciliation and peaceful coexistence. Moreover, the realisation of purposes should be the core objective of all fundamental linguistic and rational methodologies of ijtihad, regardless of their various names and approaches. Therefore, the validity of any ijtihad should be determined based on its level of achieving 'purposefulness,' or realising *maqāṣid al-sharīʿah*.

NOTES

1. Mohammad al-Tahir ibn Ashur, *Ibn Ashur, Treatise on Maqāṣid al-Sharīʿah*, trans. Muhammad el-Tahir el-Mesawi (London, Washington: International Institute of Islamic Thought (IIIT), 2006), p.2.
2. Rudolf von Jhering, *Law as a Means to an End* (Der Zweck im Recht), trans. Isaac Husik, 2nd reprint ed. (New Jersey: The Lawbook Exchange [Originally published 1913 by Boston Book Co.], 2001), p.35.
3. Ibn Ashur, *Maqāṣid al-Sharīʿah al-Islāmiyyah*, ed. el-Tahir el-Mesawi (Kuala Lumpur: al-Fajr, 1999), p.183.
4. ʿAbdul-Malik al-Juwaynī, *Ghīath al-Umam fī Iltiyāth al-Ẓulam*, ed. Abdul-Azim al-Deeb (Qatar: Wazarah al-Shu'ūn al-Dīniyyah, 1400 AH) p.253.
5. Abū Ḥāmid al-Ghazālī, *al-Mustaṣfā fī ʿIlm al-Uṣūl*, ed. Mohammed Abdul-Salam Abdul Shafi, 1st ed. (Beirut: Dār al-Kutub al-ʿIlmiyyah, 1413 AH), vol. 1, p.172.
6. Abū Bakr al-Mālikī ibn al-ʿArabī, *al-Maḥṣūl fī Uṣūl al-Fiqh*, ed. Hussain Ali Alyadri and Saeed Foda, 1st ed. (Amman: Dār al-Bayāriq, 1999), vol. 5, p.222. Al-Āmidī, ʿAlī Abū al-Ḥasan, *al-Iḥkām fī Uṣūl al-Aḥkām*. (Beirut: Dār al-Kitāb al-ʿArabī, 1404 AH), vol. 4, p.286.
7. Najm al-Dīn al-Ṭūfī, *al-Taʿyīn fī Sharḥ al-Arbaʿīn* (Beirut: al-Rayyān, 1419 AH), p.239.
8. Shihāb al-Dīn al-Qarāfī, *al-Dhakhīrah* (Beirut: Dār al-ʿArab, 1994), vol. 5, p.478.
9. Al-Ghazālī, *al-Mustaṣfā*, vol. 1, p.172, Ibn al-ʿArabī, *al-Maḥṣūl fī Uṣūl al-Fiqh,* vol. 5, p.222, al-Āmidī, *al-Iḥkām*, vol. 4, p.287.
10. Al-Ghazālī, *al-Mustaṣfā*, vol. 1, p.172, Ibrāhīm al-Ghirnāṭī al-Shāṭibī, *al-Muwāfaqāt fī Uṣūl al Sharīʿah*, ed. Abdullah Diraz (Beirut: Dār al-Maʿrifah, no date), vol. 3, p.47.
11. Al-Shāṭibṭī, *al-Muwāfaqāt*, vol. 3, p.5.

12. Ibid., vol. 1, p.151.
13. Gamal Attia, *Naḥwa Tafʿīl Maqāṣid al-Sharīʿah* (Amman: al-Maʿhad al-ʿĀlamī li al-Fikr al-Islāmī, 2001) p.45.
14. A. H. Maslow, "A Theory of Human Motivation," *Psychological Review*, no. 50 (1943): 50, pp.370–96.
15. A. H. Maslow, *Motivation and Personality*, 2nd ed. (New York: Harper and Row, 1970), Maslow, "*A Theory of Human Motivation.*"
16. According to a discussion with Shaykh Hasan al-Turabi (Oral Discussion, Khartoum, Sudan, August 2006).
17. Numan Jughaim, *Ṭuruq al-Kashf ʿan Maqāṣid al-Shāriʿ* (International Islamic University, Malaysia. Published by Dār al-Nafā'is, 2002), pP.26–35.
18. Mohammad Rashid Rida, *al-Waḥī al-Moḥammadī: Thubūt al-Nubuwwah bi al-Qur'ān* (Cairo: Mu'asasah ʿIzz al-Dīn, no date) p.100.
19. Ibn Ashur, *Maqāṣid al-Sharīʿah al-Islāmiyyah*, p.183.
20. As in, for example, Kamāl al-Dīn al-Siwāsī, *Sharḥ Fatḥ al-Qādir*, 2nd ed. (Beirut: Dar al-Fikr, no date), vol.4, p.513.
21. For example, Surah *al-Kahf*, 18:29.
22. Mohammad al-Tahir ibn Ashur, *Uṣūl al-Niẓām al-Ijtimāʿī fī al-Islām*, ed. Mohammad el-Tahir el-Mesawi (Amman: Dār al-Nafā'is, 2001) p.256, 268.
23. Ibid, pp.270–281.
24. Gamal Attia, *Naḥwa Tafʿīl Maqāṣid al-Sharīʿah*, (Amman: al-Maʿhad al-ʿĀlamī li al-Fikr al-Islāmī, 2001), p.49.
25. Mawil Izzi Dien, *Islamic Law: From Historical Foundations to Contemporary Practice*, ed., Carole Hillenbrand (Edinburgh: Edinburgh University Press Ltd, 2004), pp.131–132.
26. Yusuf al-Qaradawi, *Kayf Nataʿāmal Maʿa al-Qur'ān al-ʿAẓīm?*, 1st ed. (Cairo: Dār al-Shorūq, 1999).
27. Oral Discussions, London, UK, March, 2005, and Sarajevo, Bosnia, May, 2007.
28. Taha Jabir al-Alwani, *Maqāṣid al-Sharīʿah*, 1st ed. (Beirut: IIIT and Dār al-Hādī, 2001), p.25.
29. Oral Discussion, Cairo, Egypt, April, 2007.
30. Around the seventh Islamic year AH. The location was a few miles away from Madinah.
31. Moḥammad al-Bukhārī, *al-Ṣaḥīh*, ed. Mustafa al-Bagha, 3rd ed. (Beirut: Dār ibn Kathīr, 1986) vol. 1, p.321, Abū al-Ḥussain Muslim, *Ṣaḥīh Muslim*, ed. Mohammad Fouad Abdul-Baqi (Beirut: Dār Iḥyā' al-Turāth al-ʿArabī, no date) vol. 3, p.1391.
32. Narrated by ʿAbdullāh ibn ʿUmar, according to al-Bukhārī, vol. 1, p.321, and Muslim, vol. 3, p.1391.

33. ʿAlī ibn Ḥazm, *al-Muḥallā*, ed. Lajnah Iḥyā' al-Turāth al-ʿArabī, 1st ed. (Beirut: Dār al-Āfāq, no date), vol. 3, p.291.
34. Yaʿqūb Abū Yūsuf, *al-Kharāj* (Cairo: al-Maṭbaṭʿah al-Amīriyyah, 1303 AH) p.14, 81, Yaḥyā ibn Ādam, *al-Kharāj* (Lahore, Pakistan: al-Maktabah al-ʿIlmiyyah, 1974) p.110.
35. The Qur'an, Surah *al-Hashr*, 59:7. I preferred 'domination of wealth' to express '*dūlatan bayn al-ghaniyyā'i minkom*,' rather than 'a circuit between the wealthy' (as in Yusuf Ali's translation) or 'commodity between the rich' (as in Picktall's translation).
36. Mohammad Biltaji, *Manhaj ʿUmar Ibn al-Khaṭṭāb fī al-Tashrīʿ*, 1st ed. (Cairo: Dār al-Salām, 2002) p.190.
37. Al-Walīd ibn Rushd (Averröes), *Bidāyah al-Mujtahid wa Nihāyah al-Muqtaṣid* (Beirut: Dār al-Fikr, no date), vol. 1, p.291.
38. Al-Siwāsī, Kamāl al-Dīn, *Sharḥ Fatḥ al-Qādir*, vol. 2, p.192, Abū ʿUmar ibn ʿAbd al-Barr, *al-Tamhīd*, ed. Mohammad al-Alawi and Mohammad al-Bakri (Morrocco: Wazārah ʿUmūm al-Awqāf, 1387 AH), vol. 4, p.216.
39. Yusuf al-Qaradawi, "Fiqh al-Zakah" (Ph.D. diss, al-Azhar University, Egypt, Published by *al-Risālah*, 15th ed, 1985), vol. 1, p.229.
40. Opinion strongly expressed in: ʿAlī ibn Ḥazm, *al-Muḥallā*, ed. Lajnah Iḥiyā' al-Turāth al-ʿArabī, 1st ed. (Beirut: Dār al-Āfāq, no date) *al-Muḥallā*, p.209.
41. Al-Qaradawi, "Fiqh al-Zakah," vol. 1, pp.146–148.
42. Al-Bukhārī, *al-Ṣaḥīḥ*, *Kitāb al-Ḥajj*, *Bāb al-Raml*.
43. Al-Shāṭibī, *al-Muwāfaqāt*, vol. 2, p.6.
44. According to Ahmad al-Raysuni, *Naẓariyyat al-Maqāṣid ʿind al-Imām al-Shāṭibī*, 1st ed. (Herndon, VA: IIIT, 1992).
45. Also according to Ahmad al-Raysuni, in: Mohamed Saleem el-Awa, ed., *Maqāṣid al-Sharīʿah al-Islāmiyyah: Dirāsāt fī Qaḍāyā al-Manhaj wa Qaḍāyā al-Taṭbīq* (Cairo: al-Furqān Islamic Heritage Foundation, al-Maqāṣid Research Centre, 2006), p.181.
46. Mohammad Kamal Imam, *al-Dalīl al-Irshādī Ilā Maqāṣid al-Sharīʿah al-Islāmiyyah* (London: al-Maqāṣid Research Centre, 2007), Introduction, p.3.
47. I learnt about the book from Professor Ahmad al-Raysuni of the Organization of Islamic Conference (OIC), Fiqh Council, in Jeddah (Oral Conversation, Jeddah, Saudi Arabia, April 2006). I obtained a microfilm of the manuscript with the help of Professor Ayman Fouad, who edits manuscripts for Al-Furqan Islamic Heritage Foundation, London, UK (Cairo, July 2006). Al-Qaffāl al-Shāshī, "Maḥāsin al-Sharā'iʿ," in *Fiqh Shāfiʿī*, Manuscript No. 263 (Cairo, Dār al-Kutub: 358 AH/969 CE).
48. Al-Lughani, Abd al-Nasir, "A Critical Study and Edition of the First Part of Kitab Mahasin al-Shariʿah by al-Qaffal al-Shashi."(Ph.D. diss, University of Manchester, 2004).

49. Izzi Dien, *Islamic Law*, p.106.
50. Hasan Jabir, "al-Maqāṣid fī al-Madrasah al-Shīʿiyyah," in El-Awa, Mohamed Saleem, ed. *Maqāṣid al-Sharīʿah al-Islāmiyyah: Dirāsāt fī Qaḍāyā al-Manhaj wa Qaḍāyā al-Taṭbīq* (Studies in the Philosophy of Islamic Law: Theory and Applications). 1st ed. (Cairo: al-Furqan Islamic Heritage Foundation, Al-Maqāṣid Research Centre, 2006) p.325. Also: Oral Discussion over the issue in Alexandria, Egypt, August, 2006.
51. According to Prof. Mohammad Kamal Imam of Alexandria University's Faculty of Law (Oral Discussion, Cairo, Egypt, August, 2006).
52. Ibn Bābawayh al-Ṣadūq al-Qummī, *ʿIlal al-Sharā'iʿ*, ed. Mohammad Sadiq Bahr al-Ulum (Najaf: Dār al-Balāghah, 1966).
53. According to Prof. Ahmad al-Raysuni, Oral Discussion, Jeddah, November 2006. He referred me to: Abū al-Ḥasan al-Faylasūf al-ʿĀmirī, *al-Iʿlām bi-Manāqib al-Islām*, ed. Ahmad Ghurab (Cairo: Dār al-Kitāb al-ʿArabī, 1967).
54. Oral discussion with Shaykh Bin Bayyah in Makkah, Saudi Arabia, April 2006.
55. Al-Juwaynī, Abdul-Malik, *al-Burhān fī Uṣūl al-Fiqh*, ed. Abdul-Azim al-Deeb, 4th ed. (Manṣūrah: al-Wafā', 1418 AH/1998 CE), vol. 2, p.621, 622, 747.
56. Ibid.
57. Al-Juwaynī, *Ghīath al-Umam fī Iltiyath al-Ẓulam*, ed. Abdul-Azim al-Deeb (Qatar: Wazārah al-Shu'ūn al-Dīniyyah, 1400 AH), p.434.
58. Ibid., p.490.
59. Ibid., p.446, 473, 494.
60. Al-Ghazālī, *al-Mustaṣfā* p.258.
61. Ibid., p.172.
62. Ibid., p.174.
63. Ibid., p.265.
64. Al-ʿIzz ibn ʿAbd al-Salām, *Maqāṣid al-Ṣawm*, ed. Iyad al-Tabba, 2nd ed. (Beirut: Dār al-Fikr, 1995).
65. Al-ʿIzz ibn ʿAbd al-Salām, *Qawāʿid al-Aḥkām fī Maṣāliḥ al-Anām* (Beirut: Dār al-Nashr, no date), vol. 2, p.221.
66. Ibid., vol. 2, p.160.
67. Shihāb al Dīn al-Qarāfī, *al-Furūq (Maʿa Hawāmishih)*, ed. Khalil Mansour (Beirut: Dār al-Kutub al-ʿIlmiyyah, 1998), vol. 1, p.357.
68. Ibn Ashur, *Maqāṣid al-Sharīʿah al-Islāmiyyah*, p.100.
69. Al-Qarāfī, *al-Dhakhīrah*, vol. 1, p.153. Al-Qarāfī, *al-Furūq (Maʿa Hawāmishih)*, vol. 2, p.60.
70. Shamsuddīn ibn al-Qayyim, *Iʿlām al-Muwaqqiʿīn*, ed. Taha Abdul Rauf Saad (Beirut: Dār al-Jīl, 1973), vol. 1, p.333.

71. Al-Shāṭibī, *al-Muwāfaqāt,* vol. 2, p.6.
72. Ibid., vol. 2, p.25.
73. Ibid., vol. 2, p.61.
74. Al-Raysuni, *Naẓariyyah al-Maqāṣid*, p.169.
75. Al-Shāṭibī, *al-Muwāfaqāt,* vol. 4, p.229.
76. Ibid., vol. 2, p.6.
77. For example, Shaykh Ali Jumah, Mufti of Egypt (Oral Discussion, Cairo, Egypt, December 2005).
78. Al-ʿĀmirī, *al-Iʿlām*, p.125.
79. Al-Juwaynī, *al-Burhān*, vol. 2, p.747.
80. Al-Ghazālī, *al-Mustaṣfā*, p.258.
81. Ibn Ashur, al-Tahir, *Uṣūl al-Niẓām al-Ijtimāʿī fī al-Islām*, ed. Mohammad el-Tahir el-Mesawi (Amman: Dār al-Nafā'is, 2001), p.206.
82. For example, Shaykh Ali Jumah, Mufti of Egypt (Oral Discussion, Cairo, Egypt, December 2005).
83. Jasser Auda, *Fiqh al-Maqāṣid: Ināṭah al-Aḥkām al-Sharʿiyyah bi-Maqāṣidihā* (Virginia, IIIT: al-Maʿhad al-ʿĀlamī li al-Fikr al-Islāmī, 2006), p.20.
84. Al-Bukhārī, *al-Ṣaḥīḥ*, vol. 1, p.37.
85. Yusuf al-Qaradawi, *Madkhal li-Dirāsah al-Sharīʿah al-Islāmiyyah* (Cairo: Wahba, 1997) p.101, Attia, *Naḥwa Tafʿīl Maqāṣid al-Sharīʿah*, p.170, Ahmad al-Raysuni, Mohammad al-Zuhaili, and Mohammad O. Shabeer, "Ḥuqūq al-Insān Miḥwar Maqāṣid al-Sharīʿah," *Kitāb al-Ummah*, no. 87 (2002), Mohamed el-Awa, *al-Fiqh al-Islāmī fī Ṭarīq al-Tajdīd* (Cairo: al-Maktab al-Islāmī, 1998) p.195.
86. Mohammed Osman Salih, "al-Islām Huwa Niẓām Shāmil Liḥimāyah wa Taʿzīz Ḥuqūq al-Insān" (paper presented at the International Conference on Islam and Human Rights, Khartoum, 2006).
87. University of Toronto Bora Laskin Law Library, *International Protection of Human Rights* (2004 [cited Jan. 15th, 2005]); available from http://www.law-lib.utoronto.ca/resguide/humrtsgu.htm.
88. United Nations High Commission for Human Rights UNHCHR, *Specific Human Rights Issues* (July, 2003 [cited Feb. 1st, 2005]); available from http://www.unhchr.cah/Huridocda/Huridoca.nsf/(Symbol)/E.CN.4.Sub.2.2003.NGO.15.En.
89. Ibid.
90. Salih, "al-Islām Huwa Niẓām Shāmil Liḥimāyah wa Taʿzīz Ḥuqūq al-Insān." Murad Hoffman, *al-Islām ʿĀm Alfayn* (Islam in the Year Two Thousand), 1st ed. (Cairo: Maktabah al-Shurūq, 1995) p.56.
91. Al-ʿĀmirī, *al-Iʿlām*, p.125.
92. Ibn Ashur, *Maqāṣid al-Sharīʿah al-Islāmiyyah*, p.292.

93. Attia, *Naḥwa Tafᶜīl Maqāṣid al-Sharīᶜah*, p.171, al-Raysuni, al-Zuhaili, and Shabeer, "Ḥuqūq al-Insān Miḥwar Maqāṣid al-Sharīᶜah."
94. The Qur'an, Surah *al-Baqarah*, 2:256. This is my translation for '*lā ikrāha fī al-dīn*.' I understand that it means that there is no compulsion in any matter of the religion, rather than merely 'in religion,' as in other translations (for example, Yusuf Ali's and Picktall's).
95. Quttub Sano, *Qirā'ah Maᶜrifiyyah fī al-Fikr al-Uṣūlī*, 1st ed. (Kuala Lumpur: Dār al-Tajdīd, 2005) p.157.
96. United Nation Development Programme UNDP, *Annual Report 2004* (2004 [cited Feb. 5th, 2005]); available from http://www.undp.org/annualreports/2004/english.
97. Mohammad Shakir al-Sharif, *Ḥaqīqah al-Dīmuqrāṭiyyah* (Riyadh: Dār al-Waṭan, 1992), p.3, Mohammad Ali Mufti, *Naqd al-Judhūr al-Fikriyyah li al-Dīmuqrāṭiyyah al-Gharbiyyah* (Riyadh: al-Muntadā al-Islāmī and Majallah al-Bayān, 2002), p.91.
98. Al-Ghazālī, *al-Mustaṣfā fī Uṣūl al-Fiqh*, p.279, al-Shāṭibī, *al-Muwāfaqāt*, vol. 4, p.129, Ibn Taymiyah, *Kutub wa Rasā'il wa Fatwā*, ed. Abdul-Rahman al-Najdi, 2nd ed. (Riyadh: Maktabah ibn Taymiyah, no date), vol. 19, p.131.
99. Al-Ghazālī, *Maqāṣid al-Falāsifah* (Cairo: Dār al-Maᶜārif, 1961), p.62.
100. Ibn Taymiyah, *Kutub wa Rasā'il wa Fatwā*, vol. 19, p.131.
101. Abdul-Aziz al-Bukhari, *Kashf al-Asrār* (Beirut: Dār al-Kutub al-ᶜIlmiyyah, 1997), vol. 3, p.77.
102. Etimologically, abrogation (*naskh*) is derived from the root *na sa kha*. I carried out a survey on this root and all its possible derivations in a large number of today's popular collections of hadith, including, *al-Bukhārī, Muslim, al-Tirmithī, al-Nasā'ī, Abū Dāwūd, Ibn Mājah, Aḥmad, Mālik, al-Dāramī, al-Mustadrak, Ibn Ḥibbān, Ibn Khuzaymah, al-Bayhaqī, al-Dārquṭnī, Ibn Abī Shaybah*, and *ᶜAbd al-Razzāq*. I found no valid hadith attributed to the Prophet that contains any of these derivations of the root *na sa kha*. I found about 40 instances of 'abrogations' mentioned in the above collections, which were all based on one of the narrators' opinions or commentaries, rather than any of the texts of the hadith.
103. For example, refer to Al-Rāzī, *al-Tafsīr al-Kabīr* (Beirut: Dār al-Kutub al-ᶜIlmiyyah, 2000), vol. 3, p.204, al-Faḍl ibn al-Ḥussayn al-Tubrūsī, *Majmaᶜ al-Bayān fī Tafsīr al-Qur'ān* (Beirut: Dār al-ᶜUlūm, 2005), vol. 1, p.406, Mohammad Nada, *al-Nāskh fī al-Qur'ān* (Cairo: al-Dār al-ᶜArabiyyah li al-Kutub, 1996), p.25.
104. Al-Bukhārī, *al-Ṣaḥīḥ*, p. 69.
105. Ibid.
106. Auda, *Fiqh al-Maqāṣid*, p.106.

107. Abū Bakr al-Mālikī ibn al-ᶜArabī, *ᶜĀriḍah al-Aḥwadhī* (Cairo: Dār al-Waḥy al-Moḥammadī, no date), vol. 10, p.264.
108. Trans. M. Asad.
109. Verses 2:256, 6:13, 23:96, 30:60, 41:46, 109:6, respectively. (trans. M. Asad).
110. Burhan Zuraiq, *al-Ṣaḥīfah: Mīthāq al-Rasūl*, 1st ed. (Damascus: Dār al-Numayr and Dār Maᶜad, 1996), p.353.
111. Ibid., p.216.
112. Based on the same survey of the books of hadith that I carried out, as mentioned above.
113. Taha Jabir al-Alwani, "Maqāṣid al-Sharīᶜah," in *Maqāṣid al-Sharīᶜah*, ed. Abdul-Jabbar al-Rifaie (Damascus: Dār al-Fikr, 2001) p.89.
114. As suggested by a number of jurists. For example: al-Shāfiᶜī, *al-Risālah*, pp. 272–75, Mohammad al-Zurqani, *Sharḥ al-Zurqānī ᶜAlā Muwaṭṭa' al-Imām Mālik*. 1st ed. (Beirut: Dār al-Kutub al-ᶜIlmiyyah, no date), vol. 1, p.229.
115. Al-Siwāsī, *Sharḥ Fatḥ al-Qādir*, vol. 1, p.311, al-Sarkhasī, Moḥammad ibn Aḥmad, *Uṣūl al-Sarkhasī* (Beiut: Dār al- Maᶜrifah, no date), vol. 1, p.12, al-Kassānī, ᶜAlā' al-Dīn, *Badā'iᶜ al-Ṣanā'iᶜ fī Tartīb al-Sharā'iᶜ*, 2nd ed. (Beirut: Dār al-Kitāb al-ᶜArabī, 1982), vol. 1, p.207.
116. Al-Shāfiᶜī, Moḥammad ibn Idrīs, *al-Risālah*, ed. Ahmad Shakir, (Cairo: al-Madanī, 1939), pp. 272–75.
117. Moḥammad ibn ᶜĪsā al-Tirmidhī, *al-Jāmiᶜ al-Ṣaḥīḥ Sunan al-Tirmidhī*, ed. Ahmad M. Shakir (Beirut: Dār Iḥyā' al-Turāth al-ᶜArabī, no date), vol. 2, p.275.
118. Al-Nawawī, Yaḥya Abū-Zakariyah, *al-Majmūᶜ* (Beirut: Dār al-Fikr, 1997), vol. 4, p.145.
119. Al-Ghazālī, *al-Mustaṣfā*, vol. 1, pp.172–74.
120. Ibn Ashur, *Maqāṣid al-Shariᶜah al-Islāmiyyah*, p. 236.
121. Zayn al-Dīn ibn Nujaym, *al-Baḥr al-Rā'iq*, 2nd ed. (Beirut: Dār al-Maᶜrifah, no date), vol. 3, p.117, Ali al-Mirghiyānī, *al-Hidāyah Sharḥ Bidāyah al-Mubtadi'* (al-Maktabah al Islāmiyyah, no date), vol. 1, p.197.
122. Al-Siwāsī, *Sharḥ Fatḥ al-Qādir*, vol. 3, p.258.
123. Ibn Abidin, Mohammad Amin, *Ḥāshiyah Radd al-Muḥtār* (Beirut: Dār al-Fikr, 2000), vol. 3, p.55.
124. Mohammad al-Ghazaly, *Naẓarāt fī al-Qur'ān* (Cairo: Nahḍah Miṣr, 2002), p.194.
125. al-Nīsābūrī, al-Ḥākim, *al-Mustadrak ᶜAlā al-Ṣaḥīḥayn* (Beirut: Dār al-Kutub al-ᶜIlmiyyah, 1990), vol. 2, p.255.
126. Ibn Rushd, al-Walīd, (Averröes), *Bidāyah al-Mujtahid wa Nihāyah al-Muqtaṣid* (Beirut: Dār al-Fikr, no date), vol. 2, p.43.

127. Moḥammad ibn Ismāʿīl al-Ṣanʿānī, *Subul al-Salām Sharḥ Bulūgh al-Marām Min Adilah al-Aḥkām*, ed. Mohammad Abdul Aziz al-Khouli (Beirut: Dār Ihyā' al-Turāth al-ʿArabī, 1379 AH), vol. 3, p.227.
128. Ibid.
129. Ibid.
130. Al-Ghazaly, *al-Sunnah al-Nabawiyyah Bayna Ahl al-Fiqh wa Ahl al-Ḥadīth*, 11th ed. (Cairo: Dār al-Shurūq, 1996), p.161.
131. Oral Discussion, Sarajevo, Bosnia, May 2007, 18th regular session for the European Council for Fatwa and Research.
132. Refer to Qaradawi's article in: Mohamed Saleem El-Awa, ed., *Maqāṣid al-Sharīʿah al-Islāmiyyah: Dirāsāt fī Qaḍāyā al-Manhaj wa Qaḍāyā al-Taṭbīq* (Cairo: al-Furqan Islamic Heritage Foundation, al-Maqāṣid Research Centre, 2006) pp. 117–121.
133. Taha Jabir al-Alwani, *Issues in Contemporary Islamic Thought* (London-Washington: International Institute of Islamic Thought (IIIT), 2005), pp.164–166.
134. Quotes are his. Shamsuddin, Ayatollah Medhi, *al-Ijtihād wa al-Tajdīd fī al-Fiqh al-Islāmī* (Beirut: al-Mu'assassah al-Dawliyyah, 1999), p.128.
135. Ibid., p.129.
136. El-Affendi, Abdelwahab, ed. *Rethinking Islam and Modernity: Essays in Honour of Fathi Osman* (London: Islamic Foundation, 2001), p.45.
137. Hasan al-Turabi, *Emancipation of Women: An Islamic Perspective*, 2nd ed. (London: Muslim Information Centre, 2000), p.29. Also, oral discussion, Khartoum, Sudan, August 2006.
138. Roger Garaudy, *al-Islām wa al-Qarn al-Wāḥid wa al-ʿUshrūn: Shurūṭ Nahḍah al-Muslimīn*, trans. Kamal Jadallah (Cairo: al-Dār al-ʿĀlamiyyah li al-Kutub wa al-Nashr, 1999), pp. 70, 119.
139. Soroush, Abdul-Karim, "The Evolution and Devolution of Religious Knowledge," in *Liberal Islam: A Sourcebook*, ed. Charles Kurzman (Oxford: Oxford University Press, 1998) p.250.
140. Shahrour, Mohammed, *Naḥwa Uṣūl Jadīdah li al-Fikr al-Islāmī*, Dirāsāt Islāmiyyah Muʿāṣirah. (Damascus: al-Ahalī Press, 2000), p.125.
141. Taylor, ed, *Encyclopedia of Postmodernism*, p.178, Friedrich Meinecke, *Historicism: The Rise of a New Historical Outlook*, trans. J. E. Anderson (London: 1972).
142. Abu Zaid, "Divine Attributes in the Qur'an," in *Islam and Modernity: Muslim Intellectuals Respond*, ed. John Cooper, Ronald L. Nettler and Mohamed Mahmoud (London: I.B.Tauris, 1998), p.199, Arkoun, Mohamed, "Rethinking Islam Today," in *Liberal Islam: A Sourcebook*, edited by Charles Kurzman. (Oxford: Oxford University Press, 1998), p.211.

143. Abu-Zaid, Nasr Hamed, *al-Imām al-Shāfiʿī wa Ta'sīs al-Āīdyūlūjiyyah al-Wasaṭiyyah,* 3rd ed. (Cairo: Madbūlī, 2003), p.209, Ebrahim Moosa, "The Debts and Burdens of Critical Islam," in *Progressive Muslims*, ed. Omid Safi (Oxford: Oneworld, 2003), p.114.
144. Moghissi, Haideh, *Feminism and Islamic Fundamentalism: The Limits of Postmodern Analysis* (New York: Zed Books, 1999), p.141.
145. Ibid, p.140.
146. Ibn Warraq, "Apostasy and Human Rights," *Free Inquiry*, Feb/March 2006 no date, p.53.
147. Moosa, "Introduction," in *Revival and Reform in Islam: A Study of Islamic Fundamentalism by Fazlur Rahman*, ed. Ebrahim Moosa (Oxford: OneWorld, 2000, p.42.
148. Hasan al-Turabi, *al-Tafsīr al-Tawḥīdī*, 1st ed., vol. 1 (London: Dār al-Sāqī, 2004), p.20, Hasan Mohamed Jabir, *al-Maqāṣid Alkuliyyah wa al-Ijtihād Almuʿāṣir-Ta'sīs Manhaji wa Qur'ānī li Āliyyah al-Isṭinbāṭ*, 1st ed. (Beirut: Dār al-Ḥiwār, 2001), p.35.
149. For example al-Alwani, Taha Jabir, "Madkhal Ilā Fiqh al-Aqalliyyāt." Paper presented at the European Council for Fatwa and Research, ECFR, Dublin, Jan. 2004, p.36, al-Ghazaly, *al-Sunnah al-Nabawiyyah*, pp. 19, 125, 61, al-Ghazaly, *Naẓarāt fī al-Qur'ān*, p. 36, Abdul-Moneim al-Nimr, *al-Ijtihād* (Cairo: Dār al-Shurūq, 1986), p.147, Hasan al-Turabi, *Qaḍāyā al-Tajdīd: Naḥwa Manhaj Uṣūlī* (Beirut: Dār al-Hādī, 2000), p.157, Yassin Dutton, *The Origins of Islamic Law: The Qur'an, the Muwaṭṭa' and Madinan ʿAmal* (Surrey: Curzon, 1999) p.1, John Makdisi, "A Reality Check on Istihsan as a Method of Islamic Legal Reasoning," *UCLA Journal of Islamic and Near Eastern Law*, no. 99 (fall/winter) (2003), A. Omotosho, "The Problem of al-Amr in Usul al-Fiqh" (Ph.D. diss, University of Edinburgh, 1984), Luay Safi, *IʿMāl al-ʿAql* (Pittsburgh: Dār al-Fikr, 1998), p.130, Shamsuddin, *al-Ijtihād wa al-Tajdīd fī al-Fiqh al-Islāmī*, p.21.
150. Ibn Ashur, *Maqāṣid al-Sharīʿah al-Islāmiyyah*, Chapter 6.
151. I referred here to Mohamed al-Tahir Mesawi's translation of Ibn Ashur's book on *Maqāṣid*: Mohammad al-Tahir ibn Ashur, *Ibn Ashur Treatise on Maqāṣid al-Shariʿah*, trans. Mohamed El-Tahir El-Mesawi (London-Washington: International Institute of Islamic Thought [IIIT], 2006).
152. al-Shawkānī, Moḥammad ibn ʿAlī, *Irshād al-Fuḥūl Ilā Taḥqīq ʿIlm al-Uṣūl*, ed. Mohammed Said al-Badri, 1st ed. (Beirut: Dār al-Fikr, 1992), p. 246, Abu Zahrah, Mohammad, *Uṣūl al-Fiqh* (Cairo: Dār al-Fikr al-ʿArabī, 1958), p.268.
153. Abu Zahrah, *Uṣūl al-Fiqh*, p.271.
154. Al-Shāṭibī, *al-Muwāfaqāt*, vol. 2, p.249.

155. AbuZahrah, *'Uṣūl al-Fiqh*, p.273.
156. Ibid., p.273.
157. Wolfe, Robert Paul, *About Philosophy*, 8th ed. (New Jersey: Prentice-Hall, 2000), p. 90.
158. Wajanat Abdurahim Maymani, *Qāʿidah al-Dhara'iʿ*, 1st ed. (Jeddah: Dār al-Mujtamaʿ, 2000), pp. 608, 22, 32, 50.
159. Copied from Khalid Abou El-Fadl, *Speaking in God's Name* (Oxford: Oneworld Publications, 2003), p.275.
160. Al-Qarāfī, *al-Dhakhīrah*, vol. 1, p.153. Al-Qarāfī, *al-Furūq (Maʿa Hawāmishih)*, vol. 2, p.60, Burhān al-Dīn ibn Farḥūn, *Tabṣirah al-Hukkām fī Uṣūl al-Aqḍiyah wa Manāhij al-Aḥkām*, ed. Jamal Marashli (Beirut: Dār al-Kutub al-ʿIlmiyyah, 1995), vol. 2, p.270.
161. Al-Qarāfī, *al-Dhakhīrah*, vol. 1, p.153. Al-Qarāfī, *al-Furūq (Maʿa Hawāmishih)*, vol. 2, p.60.
162. Ibn Farḥūn, Burhān al-Dīn, *Tabṣirah al-Hukkām fī Uṣūl al-Aqḍiyah wa Manāhij al-Aḥkām*, ed. Jamal Marashli (Beirut: Dār al-Kutub al-ʿIlmiyyah, 1995), vol. 2, p.270ff.
163. Al-Mubarak al-Jazri, *al-Nihāyah fī Gharīb al-Ḥadīth wa al-Athar* (Beirut: al-Maktabah al-ʿIlmiyyah, 1979), vol. 3, p.216.
164. Ibn Ashur, *Maqāṣid al-Shariʿah al-Islāmiyyah*, p.234.
165. Ibn Ashur mentioned, for example: 'Now [as for you, O Mohammad,] We have not sent you otherwise than to mankind at large' (34:28), 'Say [O Mohammad]: "O mankind! Verily, I am an Apostle to all of you"' (7:158), and the hadith: 'An apostle used to be sent specifically to his own people, while I have been sent to all of mankind' (Muslim).
166. Ibn Ashur, *Maqāṣid al-Sharīʿah al-Islāmiyyah*, p. 236.
167. For example, refer to Mohammad Mehdi Shamsuddin, "Maqāṣid al-Sharīʿah," Mohammad Hussain Fadlullah, "Maqāṣid al-Sharīʿah," al-Alwani, "Maqāṣid al-Sharīʿah," and Abdulhadi al-Fadli, "Maqāṣid al-Sharīʿah," in *Maqāṣid al-Sharīʿah*, ed. Abduljabar al-Rufaʿi (Damascus: Dār al-Fikr, 2001). Also refer to Qaradawi's *Madkhal.*
168. Shamsuddīn, "Maqāṣid al-Sharīʿah," p.26.
169. Wayne Grudem, *Systematic Theology* (Leicester and Grand Rapids: Inter-Varsity Press and Zondervan Publishing House, 1994, 2000), p.21.
170. Ibid. p. 22.
171. For example, Ibid. p.67, 65, 110, 119, 123, 135, 143, 164, 172, 189, 208.
172. Charles Hodge, *Systematic Theology*, edited by Edward Gross (New Jersey: P & R Publishers, 1997), p.26.
173. Louis Berkhof, *Systematic Theology* (Grand Rapids: Wm. B. Eerdmans, 1996), p.15.

174. Roger Olson, *The Mosaic of Christian Beliefs: Twenty Centuries of Unity & Diversity* (Downers Grove: InterVarsity Press, 2002), p.74.
175. Charles Hodge, *Systematic Theology*, pp.24–25.
176. Al-Ghazālī, *al-Mustaṣfā*, vol. 1, p.172, Ibn al-ʿArabī, Abū Bakr al-Mālikī, *al-Maḥsūl fī Uṣūl al-Fiqh*, ed. Hussain Ali Alyadri and Saeed Foda, 1st ed. (Amman: Dār al-Bayāriq, 1999), vol. 5, p.222. Al-Āmidī, *al-Iḥkām*, vol. 4, p.287.
177. Wayne Grudem, *Systematic Theology*, p.124, 208, 241, 781, 1009.